Mrs. D. C. Weston

Jewish Antiquities, Geographical, Domestic, Political, and Religious

A Catechism for the Use of Sunday-Schools

Mrs. D. C. Weston

Jewish Antiquities, Geographical, Domestic, Political, and Religious
A Catechism for the Use of Sunday-Schools

ISBN/EAN: 9783337233709

Printed in Europe, USA, Canada, Australia, Japan

Cover: Foto ©Paul-Georg Meister /pixelio.de

More available books at **www.hansebooks.com**

JEWISH ANTIQUITIES,

GEOGRAPHICAL, DOMESTIC, POLITICAL, AND RELIGIOUS:

A Catechism,

FOR THE

USE OF SUNDAY-SCHOOLS.

BY

MRS. D. C. WESTON,

AUTHOR OF
"SYNOPSIS OF THE BIBLE" AND "CALVARY CATECHISM," ETC.

NEW YORK:
Gen. Prot. Episc. S. S. Union and Church Book Society,
762 BROADWAY.
1866

CONTENTS.

LESSON		PAGE
I.	Geography of the Holy Land	5
II.	Mountains of Palestine	7
III.	Deserts	10
IV.	Lakes of Palestine	12
V.	Fountains and pools	14
	Climate of Palestine	16
VI.	Domestic antiquities	17
VII.	Dress of the Jews	19
VIII.	Food of the Jews	21
IX.	Salutations	24
	Amusements	25
X.	Marriage	27
XI.	Education of children	29
XII.	Servants and slaves	31
XIII.	Laws concerning strangers	33
XIV.	Aged, deaf, and blind persons	36
XV.	Genealogies	38
XVI.	Treaties, oaths, etc.	40
XVII.	Covenants	43
	Oaths	44
XVIII.	Mode of computing time	46
XIX.	Mode of computing time—continued	48
XX.	Literature	51
XXI.	Music and musical instruments	53
XXII.	Arts and sciences	55
XXIII.	Carving and painting	58
XXIV.	Agriculture	60
	Commerce	61

CONTENTS.

LESSON		PAGE
XXV.	Measures	62
XXVI.	Coin	65
XXVII.	Diseases named in the Bible	67
XXVIII.	Treatment of the dead	70
XXIX.	Funerals of the Jews	72
XXX.	Political antiquities	75
XXXI.	Judges of Israel, and kings	77
XXXII.	Kings and officers of the court	80
XXXIII.	Kings—continued	83
XXXIV.	Kings of Israel and Judah	85
XXXV.	Kings of Judah	88
XXXVI.	Jewish courts of justice	90
XXXVII.	Trials	93
XXXVIII.	Punishments	95
XXXIX.	Military antiquities	97
XL.	Armies of the Jews	100
XLI.	Armies—continued	102
XLII.	Sacred antiquities	105
XLIII.	Solomon's Temple	108
XLIV.	Temple—continued	110
XLV.	Synagogues	112
XLVI.	Sacred seasons, Passover, etc.	115
XLVII.	Feast of Pentecost, etc.	118
LVIII.	Day of Atonement, etc.	120
XLIX.	Sabbatical year, etc.	123
L.	Ministers of the Temple	125
LI.	Members of the Jewish Church	127
LII.	Sacrifices	130
LIII.	Sacrifices—continued	132
LIV.	Vows and prayers	134
LV.	Purifications	137
LVI.	Idolatries of the Jews	140
LVII.	Jewish sects	143
LVIII.	Jewish sects—concluded	145

JEWISH ANTIQUITIES.

Lesson First.

GEOGRAPHY OF THE HOLY LAND.

Question. What are the principal countries mentioned in Scripture?

Answer. Palestine, Assyria, Chaldea, Phœnicia, Arabia, Asia Minor, Persia, Egypt, Ethiopia, and Media.

Q. Where are these countries situated?

A. In the western part of the continent of Asia, except Egypt, which is in Africa.

Q. How is Egypt separated from the other countries?

A. By the Red Sea, now called the Arabian Gulf.

Q. Where is it supposed the garden of Eden was situated?

A. Some persons think it was in Armenia, near the river Euphrates; others, that it was on the Imaus or Caucasian mountains.

Q. What names were given to the Holy Land?

A. The Land of Canaan, the Land of Israel, the Land of Promise, and Palestine. *Exod.* xv. 14.

Q. What was the extent of the Holy Land?

A. It was about two hundred miles from north to south, and about ninety miles broad.

Q. How was it bounded?

A. On the north by Cœlo-Syria, east by Arabia Deserta, west by the Mediterranean Sea, and on the south by Arabia Petrea.

Q. What is the principal river of Palestine?

A. The river Jordan.

Q. Where does the river Jordan rise?

A. It rises in the mountains of Libanus, flows through Lake Merom, and then through the Sea of Galilee, and empties into the Dead Sea.*

Q. What is said of the current of the Jordan?

A. It is so rapid that it does not mingle with the waters of the lake of Galilee, but goes directly through it.

Q. What other smaller rivers are there in Palestine?

---

* Jahn's Biblical Archæology, p. 18.

JEWISH ANTIQUITIES. 7

A. The Arnon, Sihor, Jabbok, Kanah, Besor, Kishon, and Cedron, or Kedron.

Q. What other river is quite celebrated?

A. The river Belus, which empties into the Mediterranean Sea.

Q. For what purpose was the sand of its banks used?

A. For the manufacture of glass; and it is said that the making of glass originated there.*

Lesson Second.

MOUNTAINS OF PALESTINE.

Q. What are the principal ranges of mountains in Palestine?

A. The mountains of Lebanon, Hermon, Engedi, Gilboa, Abarim, Gilead, and the mountains of Israel and Judah.

Q. What other mountains are celebrated in Scripture?

A. Mounts Sinai, Carmel, Nebo, Tabor, Gerizim, Ebal, Mount Moriah, and the Mount of Olives.

Q. What are the mountains of Lebanon now called?

---

* Jahn, p. 21.

A. Libanus and Anti-Libanus.

Q. What is said of these mountains?

A. They are peopled and well cultivated, and well watered, but their summits are covered with snow.

Q. For what were these mountains celebrated?

A. For the stately cedar-trees which grew upon them.

Q. How large did they grow?

A. Many of them were twelve feet in diameter, which is thirty-six feet in circumference.

Q. What are the principal peaks of the mountains of Abarim? *Deut.* xxxii. 49; xxxiv. 1.

A. Pisgah and Nebo.

Q. What remarkable valleys are mentioned in Scripture?

A. The Valley of Siddim, which was the site of the cities of Sodom and Gomorrah, is one of the most noted.

Q. Mention another, in the same chapter.

A. The valley of Shaveh, where Melchisedek met Abraham after the defeat of the confederate kings.

Q. What valley is spoken of in Joshua x. 12?

A. The Valley of Ajalon, celebrated as the place where Joshua commanded the sun and moon to stand still.

Q. What valley is spoken of in 2 Kings, xxiii. 10?

A. The Valley of Hinnom, which was celebrated for the idolatrous worship of Moloch. 2 *Chron.* xxviii. 3.

Q. What sacrifices were offered to Moloch?

A. Parents sacrificed their children by making them pass through the fire. 2 *Kings*, xxiii. 10.

Q. What was the spot called where the victims were burned?

A. Tophet.

Q. What other valleys of less note are mentioned?

A. The Valley of Blessing, the Valley of Mamre, the Valley of Bochim, the Valley of Jehoshaphat, and the Vale of Sharon.

Q. What plain is spoken of in Judges, vi. 33?

A. The Plain of Jezreel, the eastern portion of which is called Sharon, and the western, Megiddo. 2 *Kings*, ix. 27.

Q. What plain is near the lake of Gennesaret?

A. The Plain of Jericho, which is eight miles long, and two and a quarter miles wide.

Q. What plains are spoken of in Numbers, xxvi. 3?

A. The Plains of Moab, in which the Hebrews pitched their tents.

Q. What did Moses and Eleazar the priest in this plain?

A. They numbered the children of Israel a second time. *Num.* xxvi. 4.

Lesson Third.

DESERTS.

Q. To what places did the Jews give the name of desert or wilderness.

A. To places that were not cultivated, but were used as grazing places for cattle.

Q. How many classes of deserts are there in Palestine?

A. Two; some are mountainous and well watered; others are sterile, sandy plains.

Q. What was the largest of all the deserts?

A. The desert of Arabia, called the Great Desert.

Q. Where was this desert?

A. Between the Red Sea and the Land of Canaan.

Q. For what was this desert noted?

A. The Israelites sojourned in it forty years after their departure from Egypt.

Q. How is this desert described in Deuteronomy, viii. 15?

A. As "that great and terrible wilderness, wherein were fiery serpents, scorpions, and drought."

Q. Where is the Wilderness of Shur?

A. It lay towards the northeastern point of the Red Sea.

Q. Who wandered in this wilderness?

A. Hagar and her child, when driven from Abraham's tent by Sarah.

Q. Who else passed through the Wilderness of Shur?

A. The Israelites, after they had passed through the Red Sea. *Exod.* xv. 22.

Q. Where is the Wilderness of Paran?

A. It is south of Shur, in Arabia Petræa.

Q. Whom did Moses send into the Wilderness of Paran? *Num.* xiii. 3, 17.

A. He sent spies to bring intelligence concerning the land of Canaan.

Q. Where was the Desert of Sinai?

A. It was near Mount Sinai, in Arabia.

Q. What events occurred in the Desert of Sinai?

A. The Israelites encamped there, and received the chief part of the Laws of God through the ministry of Moses.

Q. Where is the Desert of Ziph?

A. Near a village of the same name, where David concealed himself from the persecution of Saul.

Q. What was the most celebrated of the eastern deserts?

A. The Wilderness or Desert of Judea.

Q. For what was it noted?

A. John the Baptist abode there, and there he preached and baptized.

Q. Who else was in that desert forty days?

A. Our Lord fasted there forty days and nights, and was tempted of the devil.

Q. Where was this desert?

A. It was south of Jerusalem, and west of the Dead Sea.

Q. What was the character of the Desert of Judea?

A. It was mountainous and wooded, but was thinly inhabited.

Lesson Fourth.

LAKES OF PALESTINE.

Q. What are the principal lakes in and near Palestine?

A. The Red Sea, the Dead Sea, the Lake of Galilee, Lake Merom, and the Great Sea.

Q. What was the Great Sea?

A. The Mediterranean Sea.

Q. What sea is spoken of in Numbers, xxi. 14?

A. The Red Sea, now called the Arabian Gulf.

Q. What is its length?

A. It is fourteen hundred miles long.

Q. Where is it situated?

Q. Between Egypt and Abyssinia on the west, and Arabia on the east.

Q. For what is it noted? *Exod.* xiv. 22.

A. For the passage of the Israelites through it on dry land when they left Egypt.

Q. What was the Dead Sea formerly called?

A. The "Salt Sea," and the "Sea of the Plain." *Deut.* iii. 17.

Q. Where is the Dead Sea situated?

A. In the southern part of Judea, supposed to be over the site of the cities of Sodom and Gomorrah.

Q. What is the size of the Dead Sea?

A. It is about seventy-two miles long and nineteen wide.

Q. What is the character of its water?

A. It is salt, bitter, and nauseous, and its specific gravity is greater than that of any other water known.

Q. What other peculiarity has it?

A. A profound silence, awful as death, broods over it, and not a ripple is seen on its surface.

Q. Has this sea ever been navigated?

A. No; several attempts have been made to navigate it without success.

Q. Where is the Sea of Galilee?

A. It is north of the Dead Sea, on the eastern border of that division of Palestine through which the Jordan flows.

Q. What was the Sea of Galilee also called?

A. The Sea of Chineroth, the Lake of Genesareth, and the Sea of Tiberias.

Q. What is the size of the Sea of Galilee?

A. It is fifteen miles long and six miles wide.

Q. What do travellers say of its waters?

A. That they are "pure as crystal, cool, sweet, and refreshing to the taste."

Q. What is said of the fish that are found in it?

A. "They are different from those found elsewhere."*

Q. What lake is mentioned in Joshua, xi. 5?

A. "The waters of Merom."

Q. What lake is this supposed to be?

A. The lake now called Houle, north of the Sea of Galilee, sixty furlongs long and thirty wide.

Lesson Fifth.

FOUNTAINS AND POOLS.

Q. What remarkable fountains or wells are mentioned in Scripture?

A. The Fountain or Pool of Siloam and Jacob's Well.

Q. What was the Pool of Siloam?

A. It was a fountain under the walls of Jerusalem, between the city and the brook Kedron.

Q. Describe this fountain.

A. It is a spring of cool, clear water, which issues from a rock and runs into a reservoir.

---

* Horne's Introduction, vol. ii., p. 27.

Q. How deep is the pool?

A. It is ten or twelve feet deep, and the descent into it is by means of fifteen or sixteen steps.

Q. What do modern travellers say of this pool?

A. They say that many persons bathe their eyes with the water of this fountain, in memory of the miracle there performed by Christ on the man born blind.

Q. With what was this pool supposed to be identical?

A. It is supposed to be the same as the fountain of En-Rogel (*Joshua*, xv. 7), and Shiloah (*Isaiah*, viii. 6)

Q. On what occasion did the Jews draw water from this fountain?

A. At the Feast of Tabernacles they brought water from it in a golden pitcher, into the Temple, and poured it, mixed with wine, upon the sacrifice as it lay upon the altar.

Q. Where was Jacob's Well?

A. It was near the city of Sychar, and it is one hundred and five feet deep.

Q Why is this well an object of great interest to Christians who visit it?

A. From the memorable discourse of our Saviour with the woman of Samaria. *John*, iv. 5.

CLIMATE OF PALESTINE

Q. What is the climate of Palestine?

A. From April until September it is excessively hot and dry, and there is no rain or thunder.

Q. When does the rainy season commence?

A. In October; and in November the leaves fall from the trees.

Q. What is said of the winters of Palestine?

A. From December until April it is quite cold, and snows are not unfrequent; thunder and lightning and hail are very common.

Q. What is said of earthquakes?

A. Earthquakes are common; also inundations of the rivers.

Q. What wind is very terrible in Palestine?

A. A violent wind called by the Arabs Simoom, and by the Turks Samyel, which blows in the summer months.

Q. What are its duration and effect?

A. It blows but seven or eight minutes, but destroys all persons whom it passes if they stand erect; they fall dead, and soon after turn black.

Q. What do travellers when they see it approaching?

A. They fall on their faces and hold their breaths so as not to inhale it.*

---

* Jahn, p. 28

Lesson Sixth.

DOMESTIC ANTIQUITIES.

Q. In what did mankind first dwell?

A. They lived in caves and tents. *Gen.* iv. 20; xix. 30.

Q. How were tents made?

A. The small tents were sustained by three poles, and covered with cloth made of wool and camel's hair.

Q. How were the larger tents made?

A. They were sustained by seven or nine poles, and covered with a black cloth made of goat's hair.*

Q. How were tents frequently pitched?

A. In a circle, and the cattle and flocks at night were driven into the inclosure.

Q. How were tents divided?

A. They were divided into three parts by means of curtains: one part for the men, one for the women, and the other for the servants.

Q. What did they build in later times?

A. They built houses of mud, wood, stone, and brick.

Q. How were bricks made in those days?

A. Of a mixture of straw and clay baked in the sun.

---

* Jahn's Arch., p. 35.

Q. What was the consistency of these bricks?

A. It was equal to that of the hardest stone.

Q. How were their houses built?

A. They were usually of but one or two stories, with a flat roof.

Q. Describe them more particularly.

A. Persons entered by a gateway a large court paved with marble, which was surrounded by a gallery.

Q. What opened from this gallery?

A. Rooms or chambers, in which the family lived.

Q. How was the court protected from the sun in summer?

A. By an awning made of vellum, stretched from one side to the other by means of ropes.

Q. How were the rooms adorned?

A. The walls of the rich were hung with velvet, the ceiling ornamented with painting and gilding, and the floors laid with painted tiles.

Q. How were they furnished?

A. With rich carpets and mats; and divans and couches on the sides of the rooms, upon which persons sat, reclined, and slept.

Q. What was their kitchen furniture?

A. It was very simple, consisting of hand-mills for grinding corn, kneading-troughs for bread, vessels of earthenware, and water-pots.

Q. What were used in the courts of princes? 1 *Kings*, x. 21.

A. Bowls, cups, and drinking-vessels of gold and silver.

Q. What did the Jews use to keep their milk, wine, and other liquors in?

A. Bottles made of skin of a red color; the mouth of the bottle was closed with a little piece of wood.

Q. How were their houses lighted?

A. With lamps filled with olive-oil.

Q. How were the streets of their cities built?

A. They were narrow, and the houses high, to protect them from the sun.

Lesson Seventh.

DRESS OF THE JEWS.

Q. With what were men first clothed?

A. With the skins of animals. *Gen.* iii. 21.

Q. As civilization advanced, what were worn?

A. Articles made of wool, flax, and silk, brilliantly dyed.

Q. What colors were most common?

A. White for cotton cloth, and purple for other material.

Q. Of what was this purple dye made?

A. It was the blood taken from a vein in the throat of a certain shell-fish, and was much esteemed.

Q. What was the common dress of the Jews?

A. A tunic of white cloth, composed of two breadths, but sometimes woven whole.

Q. With what was this tunic fastened?

A. With girdles of various kinds. The poor wore leathern girdles, those of the rich were of worsted, or silk, richly embroidered.

Q. What was worn over the tunic?

A. An upper garment, called a vest or vesture.

Q. What was the shape of the vesture?

A. It was a piece of cloth nearly square, of different sizes, from two to six yards wide.

Q. What was the Ephod?

A. It consisted of two parts, one of which was suspended over the back, the other in front, both fastened with a clasp on the shoulder; it was worn by priests and persons of high rank only.

Q. What were Phylacteries?

A. They were strips of parchment, inscribed with paragraphs taken from the law, and were tied to the arms, and sewed on the borders of garments.

Q. What coverings for the head are spoken of in Isaiah, iii. 20, 23?

A. Bonnets, hoods, and veils.

Q. What else were worn?

A. Turbans of various material, chiefly white.

Q. How was the hair worn? *Judith*, x. 3.

A. The women wore their hair long and sometimes braided, and the men wore very long beards

Q. What did they wear on their feet?

A. Sandals or soles made of wood, fastened to the feet in various ways. Sometimes they were very elegant.

Q. What ornaments did the Jewish ladies wear? *Isa.* iii. 18.

A. Rings, ear-rings, nose jewels, chains, bracelets, and tinkling ornaments on the feet and ankles.

Q. What custom was prevalent among the rich?

A. That of painting the eyelids of a dark color. *Ezek.* xxiii. 40; 2 *Kings*, ix. 30.

Q. What were the garments of mourners, on the death of friends?

A. Haircloth, sackcloth, and mourning apparel. *Gen.* xxxvii. 34; 2 *Sam.* xiv. 2.

Lesson Eighth.

FOOD OF THE JEWS.

Q. What was the principal food of the Jews?

A. It was very simple, consisting chiefly of milk,

honey, vegetables, and fruit; except at the festivals, when they ate animal food.

Q. Of what was the first bread made?

A. It was made of grain, pounded in a mortar; in later times of flour, and fermented with leaven.

Q. How did they bake their bread?

A. Cakes were baked on the hearth, but the shew-bread was baked in an oven. *Lev.* ii. 4.

Q. What were the Jews forbidden to eat?

A. All animals which had died of disease, or which had been torn by wild beasts; also animals which had been offered to idols.

Q. What else were forbidden?

A. Serpents, creeping insects, fish without scales and fins, quadrupeds which had not cloven feet and did not ruminate, and certain unclean birds.

Q. What was the ordinary beverage of the Jews?

A. Water, and wine of various sorts.

Q. What was much used in the time of Solomon?

A. Spiced wine mingled with the juice of the pomegranate.

Q. Where did the patriarchs take their meals?

A. Frequently under the shade of trees. *Gen.* xviii. 8.

Q. What did the Jews before and after eating?

A. They carefully washed their hands, and also implored the Divine blessing.

Q. At what time did the Jews take their meals?

A. They rose at dawn of day and took their breakfast, had a luncheon at eleven o'clock, and their principal meal at five or six in the evening.

Q. What was their mode of eating?

A. They had one large platter, from which all ate with their right hand.

Q. What was done after supper?

A. A cup of wine was handed to each person by the servants.

Q. Where were feasts usually given?

A. In the open halls and gardens.

Q. Did the ancient Hebrews eat with all persons?

A. No; they would not eat with any person whose religion was different from theirs.

Q. What was customary after a public feast?

A. To send a portion of what remained to those who had been prevented from coming, and also to the poor.

Q. What did travellers take with them when they journeyed?

A. They took all their provisions and every necessary, as at first there were no inns for travellers.

Q. How did they travel?

A. In caravans or companies, upon asses and camels, which carried not only their food, but household goods and merchandise.

Q. What was esteemed a sacred duty?

A. Hospitality was considered a sacred duty, and binding upon every one.

Lesson Ninth.

FORM OF SALUTATION AND AMUSEMENTS.

Q. What was the manner of salutation among the Jews?

A. Their salutations were long and tedious; the common form was, "The Lord be with thee," "Peace be with thee," with low bows, and minute inquiries after the health of the family.

Q. What was done on meeting a person of high rank?

A. They bowed to the ground and kissed the hem of his garment.

Q. How did they approach the king?

A. They prostrated themselves on the ground, and remained in that position till they were ordered to rise.

Q. What other custom was universal?

A. That of sending presents; no one ever approached an eastern prince without a present.

Q. How did relatives salute each other?

A. They kissed each other on the face, head, and neck.

Q. What was done for a guest, on his arrival?

A. Water was given him to wash his feet, and he was anointed with oil. *Gen.* xviii. 4; *Luke,* vii. 44.

Q. When a person intended visiting one of high rank, what did he do?

A. He sent previous notice, and also carried suitable presents.

Q. If a host became tired of a visitor, and desired him to depart, how did he make known his wishes?

A. He caused incense or perfumes to be burnt in the room, which was the concluding ceremony of the visit.

AMUSEMENTS.

Q. What were occasions of festivity among the Jews?

A. Weddings, the season of sheep-shearing, and harvest-home, and the birthdays of kings.*

Q. With what were these occasions accompanied?

A. With music and dancing.

Q. What practices were common in the early periods of Jewish history?

A. Military sports and exercises, the hurling of

---

* Horne's Introduction, vol. ii., p. 189.

stones from a sling, lifting stones of an enormous weight, and games of various sorts.

Q. When were these games first introduced into Jerusalem?

A. In the reign of Antiochus Epiphanes, by the profligate high-priest Jason. 2 *Macc.* iv. 9.

Q. What was also very common among the Jews?

A. Dancing was common at their feasts, in public triumphs, and at all seasons of rejoicing.

Q. On what occasion did David dance? 2 *Sam.* vi. 16.

A. When the ark of the Lord came into the city of David, King David danced before the Lord.

Q. How did Miriam also glorify God? *Exod.* xv. 20.

A. Miriam praised God in songs and dances, after the deliverance of the Israelites from Pharaoh.

Q. What do Jewish historians say of dancing?

A. That it was practised on the national festivals, and was part of the sacred worship.

Q. What instrument of music was generally used for dancing?

A. The timbrel.

Lesson Tenth.

MARRIAGE.

Q. What ceremony was preliminary to marriage?
A. The parties were solemnly betrothed.
Q. What was the betrothal?
A. It was a solemn promise of marriage made by the man and woman, each to the other, at such time as should be agreed upon.
Q. How were marriages celebrated?
A. With great festivity and splendor.
Q. With what were the bride and bridegroom adorned?
A. Sometimes with chaplets of flowers, and sometimes with crowns of gold and silver, according to their rank.
Q. What was customary among the Jews in regard to a marriage portion?
A. The wife brought a marriage portion to her husband, and the husband was obliged to give her or her parents presents of equal value.
Q. What was the marriage vow?
A. It was a covenant between the father and brothers of the bride, and the father of the bridegroom, made in the presence of witnesses.*

---

* Jahn's Archæology, p. 162.

Q. What was the usual price of a wife?

A. In the time of Moses, the medium price was thirty shekels, and the highest, fifty shekels. *Deut.* xxii. 29.

Q. How long after the betrothal did the marriage take place?

A. Usually about ten or twelve months.

Q. What were the ceremonies at the time of the marriage?

A. The bridegroom, attended by a retinue of young men, with instruments of music, conducted the bride from her father's house to his father's house.

Q. How was the bride attired?

A. She was richly adorned, and her head encircled with flowers, or with a crown of gold or silver, according to her means and rank.

Q. How was the bride attended?

A. She was attended by a company of maidens to her new home, where a feast was prepared.

Q. What else did the bridegroom prepare for the guests?

A. It was customary for the groom to prepare wedding garments, which were always white.

Q. What was the concluding ceremony?

A. The father took the hand of his daughter, placed it in the right hand of the bridegroom, and gave them his blessing.

Q. How long were the festivities continued?

A. They were frequently kept up for a week.

Q. Were daughters ever given in marriage without compensation?

A. Yes; and those who were freely given up by the father were more highly esteemed, and were themselves conscious of their superiority.

Lesson Eleventh.

EDUCATION OF CHILDREN.

Q. How was the birthday of a son regarded?

A. It was celebrated as a festival, which was solemnized every succeeding year with increasing festivity and joy.

Q. When was a son named?

A. On the eighth day, when he was also received into the Church by circumcision.

Q. What did the first-born son inherit?

A. He inherited peculiar rights and privileges; he was the ruler over his brothers and sisters, and received a double portion of the estate.

Q. How long did a son remain under the care of the mother?

A. Until his fifth year, when the father had him instructed in the arts and duties of life, and also in the Mosaic law and in religion. *Deut.* vi. 20, xi. 19.

Q. If he were to be further instructed in the sciences, what was done?

A. He was sent to some priest or Levite who had other children to instruct.

Q. What schools are spoken of in the time of Samuel?

A. There was a school near the Tabernacle, called the School of the Prophets.

Q. What else was taught to the Jewish children?

A. They were taught some trade, so that in case of misfortune they could support themselves.

Q. How were daughters educated?

A. They had no education except in domestic duties, music, singing, and dancing.

Q. Were they ever seen in public?

A. They rarely went abroad, and never without being closely covered with a veil.

Q. How was an estate divided, on the death of the father? *Deut.* xxi. 17.

A. The sons divided it equally between themselves, except that the eldest son had two portions.

Q. Could a son legally demand his portion during his father's life? *Luke*, xv. 12.

A. Yes; and the father could not refuse him.

Q. Did the daughters inherit any thing?

A. No, unless there were no sons; in which case they had the property.

Q. What were daughters usually considered?

A. They were considered part of the estate, and were sold into matrimony by their brothers.

Q. What was the law in regard to a widow?

A. The widow of the deceased, like his daughters, had no legal share in the estate, but the sons were bound to support her.

Q. If she was not satisfied with the support, what was customary?

A. She sometimes returned to her father's house. *Gen.* xxxviii. 11.

Lesson Twelfth.

SERVANTS AND SLAVES.

Q. Was slavery common among the Jews?

A. Yes, and before the time of Moses, who made various salutary laws concerning it. *Gen.* ix. 25.

Q. How were slaves acquired? *Deut.* xx. 14.

A. By captivity, and by debt, when the person was sold for payment of the debt. *2 Kings*, iv. 1.

Q. In what other way were persons made slaves?

A. By committing a theft, without the power of making restitution;* and by birth, when the children of slaves were born in the house.†

---

* Exod. xxii. 2, 3.   † Gen. xxi. 10.

Q. What was the punishment for stealing a free-born Israelite to sell him as a slave?

A. It was punished with death. *Exod.* xxi. 16.

Q. What did slaves receive from their masters?

A. Food and clothing, but of the meanest quality.

Q. If a slave lost an eye or a tooth by a blow from his master, what was the consequence?

A. He acquired his liberty.

Q. What was the consequence if a slave died by the hand of his master? *Exod.* xxi. 20.

A. The master was punished by a magistrate.

Q. What privileges had slaves? *Exod.* xx. 10.

A. They rested on the Sabbath and on the greater festivals, and were invited to certain feasts.

Q. When were all slaves freed?

A. In the year of Jubilee all were made free.

Q. If a slave of another nation fled to the Jews, how was he received?

A. He was kindly received, and on no account given up to his master. *Deut.* xxiii. 15, 16.

Q. Were slaves brought up as members of the Jewish Church?

A. Yes; and were instructed in the worship of the true God.

Q. What privileges had hired servants?

A. They rested on the Sabbath day, shared in the produce of the sabbatical year, and their wages were paid every day at sunset. *Lev.* xix. 13.

Q. What were the usual wages of a day-laborer?

A. A denarius, or fifteen cents of our money.*

Q. To what were servants entitled by law?

A. They were entitled to receive an adequate support from those for whom they worked.

Q. What length of time was a servant bound to serve one master?

A. He was not obliged to serve longer than six years; at the end of which time he was to be dismissed with presents.

Q. Were house-servants ever made heirs? *Prov.* xvii. 2.

A. A person had the right to make them his heirs if he chose to do so, and it was sometimes done.

Lesson Thirteenth.

LAWS RESPECTING STRANGERS.

Q. What two descriptions of strangers are mentioned in the laws of Moses?

A. One class were those who had no home, whether Israelites or foreigners.

---

* Horne's Introd., vol. ii., p. 167.

Q. What were the others?

A. The others were those who, though not natives, had purchased houses in Palestine.

Q. What did the Mosaic law enjoin with regard to all strangers? *Lev.* xix. 34; *Num.* ix. 14.

A. The duties of humanity and kindness were enjoined, because the Israelites themselves had once been strangers.

Q. Could strangers be naturalized?

A. Yes; by renouncing idolatry, and becoming members of the Jewish Church.

Q. What two nations were absolutely refused the right of citizenship?

A. The Ammonites and Moabites.

Q. Why?

A. Because of their bitter hostility to the Israelites while they were in the Wilderness.

Q. How were strangers treated in later times?

A. In the days of Solomon many of them were compelled to labor on religious edifices. 2 *Chron.* ii. 17, 18.

Q. Quote the passage.

A. And Solomon numbered all the strangers that were in the land of Israel, and he set threescore and ten thousand of them to be bearers of burdens, and fourscore thousand to be hewers in the mountains.

Q. From whom were these laborious services required?

A. Probably from those only who had been taken prisoners in war.

Q. What were the rights of war in regard to prisoners?

A. They could be employed in any offices, however low and laborious, which the conqueror thought proper to impose.

Q. What did the Jews understand by the word *neighbor*, in later times?

A. Their personal friends only; and they restricted their benevolence accordingly.

Q. How did our Lord illustrate their real duty?

A. By the parable of the good Samaritan.

Q. Where are beggars first mentioned?

A. They are first spoken of in the 109th Psalm, 10th verse.

Q. Where were they found in the time of Christ?

A. They usually sat near the doors of the rich, at the gates of the Temple, and in the street, but did not beg from door to door.*

Q. What peculiarity have the oriental beggars?

A. They do not ask alms as a favor, but appeal to the justice of their benefactors, and ask it as their right. *Job*, xxii. 7; *Prov.* iii. 27.

---

* Jahn's Arch., p. 197.

Lesson Fourteenth.

AGED, DEAF, AND BLIND PERSONS.

Q. What command did Moses give, concerning respect to aged persons?

A. "Thou shalt rise up before the hoary head, and honor the face of the old man." *Lev.* xix. 32.

Q. What instance is there in Scripture of the prompt and terrible punishment of those who mocked one of God's prophets? 2 *Kings,* ii. 23.

A. When the children mocked Elisha, God sent two bears, which killed forty and two of them.

Q. What statute was made in regard to deaf and blind persons? *Lev.* xix. 14.

A. "Thou shalt not curse the deaf, nor put a stumbling-block in the way of the blind."

Q. Give another text from Deuteronomy xxvii. 18.

A. "Cursed be he that maketh the blind to wander out of the way."

Q. What did Moses enjoin upon the Jews in regard to the poor? *Deut.* xv. 11.

A. "Thou shalt open wide thy hand . . . to thy poor, to thy needy, in thy land."

Q. What did he also exhort them to do for an Israelite who had become poor?

A. Not to harden their hearts, but to lend him sufficient for his need

Q. What was commanded during harvest?

A. The owner of a field or vineyard was commanded not to glean, but to 'leave what grew in the corners," and the scattered ears or sheaves, for the poor. *Lev.* xix. 9, 10.

Q. What command concerning olive-trees is found in Deuteronomy xxiv. 20?

A. After a man had shaken his olive-trees once, he was not to touch them again, so that the fruit which ripened after the season of gathering should go to the poor.

Q. What liberty was given to all, during the sabbatical year?

A. The poor had an equal right with the owners of the land to whatever grew in that year.

Q. What else were the Jews commanded to do for the poor?

A. After deducting the priests' portion of the sacrifice, the remainder was appropriated to the sacrificial feasts, to which they were bound to invite the stranger, the fatherless, and the widow.

Q. What other provision was made for the poor?

A. They received a portion of the tithes, which was expressly set apart for them.

Q. Whose business was it to look after the poor, and distribute the tithes to them?

A. That of the Levites.

Lesson Fifteenth.

GENEALOGIES.

Q. What were genealogies?

A. The history of the succession of families.

Q. Why were genealogies considered of great importance by the Jews? *Num.* xxxvi. 7.

A. Because God had commanded that the tribes should be kept distinct from each other.

Q. Who had charge of the genealogical tables?

A. The Shoterim or Scribes, of the tribe of Levi.

Q. What does Josephus say of these genealogies?

A. He says that "the Jews had an uninterrupted succession of high-priests for two thousand years."

Q. Were these genealogies preserved through the captivities?

A. Yes; they were preserved with the greatest care.

Q. What rule was made after the captivity, in case a priest could not trace his genealogy back to Abraham?

A. He was excluded from the priestly office.

Q. What genealogy did St. Luke derive from these public registers?

A. The genealogy of Christ from Adam, a period of four thousand years.

Q. What was one of the principal reasons for keeping these records so carefully?

A. It had been prophesied that Christ should be born of the tribe of Judah, and of the family of David.

Q. Upon what did the Jews pride themselves especially?

A. Upon tracing their pedigree back to Abraham.

Q. How did the Jews preserve the memory of great events in their history? *Gen.* xxxi. 45; *Josh.* iv. 20.

A. At first by raising a heap of stones on the very place where the event occurred.

Q. Did they give names to these places?

A. Yes; they gave names which indicated the nature of the transaction that had taken place.

Q. What did Moses command the Israelites to erect, after they had crossed the river Jordan?

A. An "altar of great stones, plastered with plaster," on which the laws received from God were to be inscribed.

Q. What monuments were raised in later times?

A. Fine monuments, with symbolic memorial names given them. 1 *Sam.* xv. 12; 2 *Sam.* xviii. 18.

Q. What monument did Absalom erect during his life?

A. He "reared for himself a pillar," to keep his

name in remembrance, because he had no son—and it was called Absalom's pillar.

Q. What monument is spoken of in 1st Samuel, vii. 12?

A. Samuel erected a stone at Mizpeh, to commemorate the discomfiture of the Philistines at that place.

Q. In what other way was the memory of great events perpetuated?

A. The great festivals instituted by Moses, as well as the feasts and fasts of later times, were memorials of important transactions.

Lesson Sixteenth.

TREATIES, CONTRACTS, AND OATHS.

Q. What is a treaty or covenant?

A. It is a compact or agreement between two parties.

Q. Did the Jews ever make treaties with heathen nations?

A. Yes; as in the case of Solomon with Hiram, king of Tyre (1 *Kings*, v. 12), and David with the king of Hamath. 2 *Sam.* viii. 9.

Q. Give another instance.

A. Joshua made a league with the Gibeonites. *Josh.* ix. 15.

Q. What ceremonies were used at the conclusion of a treaty?

A. Sometimes simply joining hands, sometimes raising a heap of stones. *Ezek.* xvii. 18; *Gen.* xxxi. 44, 50.

Q. What did Jacob in the latter instance? *Gen.* xxxi. 48, 54.

A. He raised a heap of stones, called the place Galeed, offered sacrifice, and made a feast for his brethren.

Q. In what way did Abraham make a covenant with the king of Gerar? *Gen.* xxi. 22, 32.

A. The covenant was ratified by the oath of both parties, by a present from Abraham to Abimelech, and by giving a name to the well which had caused the controversy.

Q. What was customary at the conclusion of a covenant?

A. They offered sacrifices and made a feast. *Gen.* xxvi. 30, 31.

Q. What covenant is spoken of in Numbers, xviii. 19?

A. "A covenant of salt." (Also, 2 *Chron.* xiii. 5.)

Q. What did that mean?

A. They deemed the eating together as a bond of perpetual friendship.

Q. Of what was salt considered an emblem?

A. It was considered an emblem of incorruptibility and permanence.

Q. What did the contracting parties on these occasions?

A. They ate together of the sacrifices offered, and the whole transaction was considered as a league of endless friendship.

Q. What was a later custom, under the Mosaic law?

A. The parties to the covenant were sometimes sprinkled with the blood of the victim sacrificed.

Q. What did the Jews in their peace-offering?

A. They feasted, in their peace-offerings, on a part of the sacrifice, in token of their reconciliation with God.

Q. Give an instance. *Exod.* xxiv. 6, 8.

A. Moses sprinkled part of the blood on the Israelites, and part of the blood on the altar, to show that God was a party to the covenant.

Q. What was this called?

A. The blood of the covenant. *Heb.* ix. 19, 20.

Q. What covenant is mentioned in Genesis, ix. 13–17?

A. God's covenant with mankind that the earth should not be again destroyed by a deluge.

Q. What was the sign of this covenant?

A. The rainbow in the heavens.

Q. What covenant did God make with Abraham?

A. That his descendants should be as the stars of heaven in multitude, and be a mighty nation. *Gen.* xxii. 17.

Q. What did God promise he would give them? *Gen.* xvii. 8.

A. The Land of Canaan for an everlasting possession.

Q. What was the whole Mosaic constitution?

A. It was a covenant between God and the Israelites.

Lesson Seventeenth.

COVENANTS AND OATHS.

Q. Where were contracts between individuals made?

A. Contracts of bargain and sale were made at the gate of the city, and the price was paid before all who went out and came in. *Ruth*, iv. 1, 2.

Q. What do we learn further from Ruth, iv. 7?

A. That in confirming the transfer of property, the proprietor took off his shoe, and gave it to the new owner.

Q. What other mode of ratifying a contract or sale is mentioned in Job, xvii. 3, and Prov. vi. 1?

A. That of joining or "striking hands."

Q. Where do we first read of written instruments, sealed and delivered? *Jer.* xxxii. 10, 12.

A. Jeremiah speaks of written instruments for the

disposal and transfer of property about six hundred years before Christ.

Q. What did Jeremiah command Baruch to do?

A. He told him to bury a document in an earthen vessel, in order to preserve it, to be produced at a future period as evidence of the purchase.

OATHS.

Q. What was the custom of the Jews in the matter of oaths?

A. Those who appealed to the Deity in attestation of any thing, held up their right hand towards heaven.

Q. What did the person making oath signify by this action?

A. He appealed to God to witness the truth of what he said.

Q. What instance is found in the Revelation of this form of taking an oath? *Rev.* x. 5.

A. The Angel of the Apocalypse "lifted up his hand to heaven, and sware by Him that liveth forever and ever."

Q. By what was an oath sometimes accompanied?

A. With an imprecation, as in Ruth, i. 17. The Lord do so unto me, and more, if aught but death part thee and me. Also, 1 *Kings*, ii. 23.

Q. What was another form of taking an oath?

A. "Let God be a witness." "As the Lord liveth." 1 *Sam.* xiv. 45.

Q. When an oath was exacted by a judge, how was it put?

A. It was put in form, and the person to whom it was put, responded by saying: "Amen, so let it be;" or, "Thou hast said." *Matt.* xxvi. 64.

Q. What other form of adjuration was common?

A. "I adjure thee by the living God" to answer whether this thing be so or not. *Matt.* xxvi. 64.

Q. Was there still another form of swearing?

A. Yes; Joseph swore "by the life of the King;" and Elisha said, "As the Lord liveth, and as thy soul liveth, I will not leave thee." 2 *Kings*, ii. 2.

Q. How were the Jews in the habit of swearing, in the time of Christ?

A. They swore by the altar, by Jerusalem, by heaven, by the gold of the Temple, and by their heads.

Q. Why did they do this? *Matt.* v. 34, 35.

A. Because the name of God was not mentioned, they considered their oaths less binding; and against this kind of **swearing** Christ expressed His displeasure.

Lesson Eighteenth.

MODE OF COMPUTING TIME.

Q. How did the Jews compute their days?

A. From evening to evening; their days commenced at six o'clock in the afternoon. *Lev.* xxiii. 32.

Q. Where is this mode first spoken of? *Gen.* i. 5.

A. In the account of the creation: "The evening and the morning were the first day."

Q. Where are hours first mentioned in Scripture?

A. In the Book of Daniel (iii. 6, 15).

Q. Who are the inventors of this division of the day?

A. The Chaldeans, from whom the Jews probably derived it.

Q. How were hours measured by the Jews? 2 *Kings*, xx. 11.

A. By the sun-dial, which was introduced from Babylon.

Q. How did the Jews compute the hours of their civil day?

A. From six in the morning till six at night.

Q. What was their first hour?

A. Their first hour corresponded with our seven,

o'clock, their second with eight, their third hour with our nine o'clock.

Q. What were the sixth, ninth, and eleventh hours?

A. The sixth hour was twelve at noon; the ninth was three after noon; and the eleventh was five after noon.

Q. How did they divide the night? *Mark*, xiii. 35.

A. Into four watches: "Even, midnight, cock-crowing" (which was three in the morning), "and morning."

Q. What constituted a week?

A. Seven days.

Q. What was their day of rest and Holy Day?

A. The seventh day, called the Sabbath.

Q. With what did the Sabbath correspond?

A. With our Saturday.

Q. What was their first day?

A. It was what we call Sunday.

Q. What did the Jews call Sunday?

A. "One of the Sabbath;" and Monday, "two of the Sabbath;" Tuesday, "three of the Sabbath," and so on.

Q. What was Friday called?

A. "The eve of the Sabbath."

Q. What constituted a month?

A. The months of the Hebrews were lunar months, and consisted of twenty-nine and thirty days alternately.

Q. Were the months and years of the Jews settled by astronomical calculations?

A. No; but by the actual appearance of the new moon: and as soon as they saw the moon they began the month.

Q. How did they fix the time?

A. Persons were appointed to watch on the tops of mountains, for the first appearance of the moon after the change; and when they saw it they informed the Sanhedrim.

Q. How was public notice given of the time? *Ps.* lxxxi. 3.

A. First, by the sounding of trumpets, and afterwards lighting beacon-fires throughout the land.

Q. What were months called, before the Deluge?

A. They had no names; but were called first month, second month, and so on. *Gen.* vii. 11; viii. 5.

Lesson Nineteenth.

COMPUTING TIME CONTINUED.

Q. How were years first regulated?

A. By the return of winter and summer.

Q. What modes existed among the Hebrews of reckoning time?

A. Two: the civil year and the sacred year.

Q. When did the civil year begin?

A. It was reckoned from the first new moon in the month Tishri—*i. e.*, October.*

Q. When did the sacred year begin?

A. On the fifteenth day of the month Nisan, or the first new moon in April. *Exod.* xii. 2, 18.

Q. Why was this?

A. To commemorate the departure of the Israelites from Egypt.

Q. Which is the more ancient reckoning?

A. The civil year, which is used only in civil and agricultural concerns.

Q. What was the first month of the sacred year called?† *Esth.* iii. 7.

A. Nisan, reckoned from the first new moon in April.

Q. What was the second month called?

A. Zif or Ziv, reckoned from new moon of May.

Q. What was the third month? *Esth.* viii. 9.

A. Sivan, reckoned from the new moon of June.

Q. What was the fourth month?

A. Tammuz, from the new moon of July.

Q. What was the fifth month?

A. Ab, from the new moon of August.

Q. What was the sixth month? *Neh.* vi. 15.

A. Elul, from the new moon of September.

---

* Jahn's Archæology, p. 112.   † Ib.

Q. What was the seventh month?

A. Tishri, the first month of the civil year, from the new moon of October.

Q. What was the eighth month? 1 *Kings*, vi. 38.

A. Bul, from the new moon of November.

Q. What was the ninth month?

A. Kislev, or Cisleu, from the new moon of December.

Q. What was the tenth month? *Esth*. ii. 16.

A. Tebeth, from the new moon of January.

Q. What was the eleventh month? *Zech*. i. 7.

A. Shebat, from the new moon of February.

Q. What was the twelfth month? *Esth*. iii. 7

A. Adar, from the new moon of March.

Q. Repeat the names of the months.

A. Nisan, Zif, Sivan, Tammuz, Ab, Elul, Tishri, Bul, Kislev, Tebeth, Shebat, Adar.

Q. What were dated from the first month of the sacred year?

A. They computed their feasts, and prophets dated their visions and oracles, from that time.

Q. What were dated from the first month of the civil year?

A. From this year the Jews dated their contracts, computed their jubilees, noted the birth of children, and the reign of kings.

Lesson Twentieth.

LITERATURE.

Q. What evidence is there that the Jews had schools for education? 2 *Kings*, xxii. 14.

A. There was a "College" at Jerusalem, and there were schools called the Schools of the Prophets. 2 *Kings*, vi. 1; iv. 38.

Q. In what were the youth instructed?

A. In religion, the knowledge of the law, and in sacred music.

Q. To what was the literature of the Jews limited?

A. To religion, the history of their nation, poetry, ethics, philosophy, and natural history.

Q. Was the art of historical writing much cultivated by the Jews?

A. Yes; as the Bible itself is an ample testimony.

Q. Was arithmetic well understood?

A. No; only the more simple methods of arithmetical calculations are spoken of in the Pentateuch.

Q. What was known of astronomy?

A. The Egyptians, Babylonians, and Phœnicians made great progress in astronomy, and from them the Jews obtained a knowledge of it.

Q. What did the Jews know of astrology?

A. Very little, as it was interdicted to the Hebrews, but it was highly esteemed among the neighboring nations.

Q. Where did the prophet Daniel study astrology?

A. In Babylon, during his captivity, but he did not practise it.*

Q. What is the character of the Hebrew poetry?

A. It has no rhyme, but is often grand, sublime, and full of pathos.

Q. Give some instances.

A. The song of Moses (Exod. xv.), David's lamentation on the death of Saul and Jonathan (2 Sam. i. 19), Hezekiah's song of praise (Isa. xxxviii.), and the prayer of Habakkuk (Hab. iii).

Q. What are there besides these single hymns?

A. The Book of Psalms, Proverbs, Ecclesiastes, Canticles, and Lamentations of Jeremiah.

Q. Where may traces of the ethics of the Jews be found?

A. In the Book of Job, Proverbs, Ecclesiastes, and the Book of Wisdom.

Q. In what study were the Jews much interested?

A. The subject of natural history.

Q. What was said of Solomon in this respect? 1 *Kings*, iv. 33.

A. That "he spake of trees, from the cedar in Lebanon to the hyssop that springeth out of the wall; and also of beasts, of fowls, of creeping things and fishes."

---

* Horne's Intro., vol. ii., p. 186.

Q. What is plainly shown in the Book of Job?

A. It is evident that the author possessed an intimate knowledge of the works of nature.

Q. Was oratory cultivated by the Jews?

A. No; not to any extent, although the sacred writers have left specimens which the most distinguished orators might imitate with advantage.

Lesson Twenty-first.

MUSIC AND MUSICAL INSTRUMENTS.

Q. Did the Jews cultivate the art of music?

A. Yes; and introduced it upon all solemn and special occasions; at public festivals and in the Temple.

Q. On what other occasions? *Judges*, xi. 34; 2 *Chron.* xxiii. 13.

A. At the coronation of their kings, and on the triumphal return of their generals after victory.

Q. What were the musical instruments of the Jews?

A. They were of two kinds, pulsatile and wind instruments.

Q. What were the pulsatile, or beaten instruments?

A. They were three in number: the tabret, the cymbal, and the sistrum.

Q. What was the tabret or timbrel?

A. It was a hoop covered with parchment, and

hung round with small bells like a modern tambourine.

Q. What was the cymbal?

A. It consisted of two plates of brass, which, being struck together, made a hollow, ringing sound.

Q. What was the sistrum?

A. It was a rod of iron bent into an oval shape, and furnished with moveable rings which were shaken or struck with a rod of iron.

Q. What wind instruments had the Jews?

A. The organ, dulcimer, horn, and trumpet, and pipes.

Q. What was the organ?

A. It is supposed to have been a kind of flute consisting of seven pipes, made of reeds of unequal length joined together.

Q. What was the dulcimer? *Dan.* iii. 5.

A. It was a wind instrument made of reeds.

Q. What was the horn?

A. It was made of the horns of oxen, cut off at the small end, and chiefly used in war.

Q. What was the trumpet?

A. It was made of metal, straight, and was used by the priests in the temple service.

Q. What were pipes?

A. They are supposed to have been the flute and hautboy.

Q. What were the stringed instruments?

A. The harp and the psaltery.

Q. What was the harp?

A. It was like a modern harp, had ten strings, and was played with the hand or a small bow.

Q. What was the psaltery?

A. It was an instrument of ten or twelve strings, in the shape of a triangle, and was played with the hand.

Q. Who had charge of the music of the temple service? *Eccles.* ii. 8.

A. The Levites sung and played upon instruments; female musicians were also admitted, and were generally the daughters of the Levites.*

Q. Who was supposed to have been the inventor of musical instruments?

A. Jubal. *Gen.* iv. 21.

Lesson Twenty-second.

ARTS AND SCIENCES.

Q. Where are any of the arts mentioned in Scripture?

A. Artificers in brass and iron, and musical instruments, in the fourth generation from Adam, are mentioned in Genesis, iv. 22.

---

* Horne's Introd., vol. ii., p. 183.

Q. What nation excelled all others, in the early ages of the world, in a knowledge of the arts?

A. Egypt; and the sojourn of the Israelites there for four hundred years taught them many things.

Q. What may illustrate this?

A. The manner in which the tabernacle was built, which was adorned with gold, silver, precious stones, and embroidery.

Q. From whom is it supposed the Jews received their alphabet?*

A. From the Phœnicians. Moses wrote the Pentateuch in Phœnician characters.

Q. Where is writing first mentioned?

A. The copy of the law, "which was written by the finger of God," is the first spoken of in Scripture.

Q. What is therefore probable?

A. It is probable that the art of writing was already understood by the Jews.

Q. What seems to have been the most ancient way of writing?

A. Engraving. "Holiness to the Lord" was engraved on a golden plate, and worn by the high-priest.

Q. Upon what did the ancient Jews write?

A. Upon tablets made of wood, covered with wax, upon which they wrote with styles of gold, or silver, or brass.

Q. What did they use in later times?

---

* Calmet's Dictionary, p. 617.

A. They used the broad flags which grew in Egypt, and leaves of palm-trees. *Isa.* xix. 7.

Q. What was afterwards used?

A. Thin parchment, made of the skins of animals, which was rolled up like a scroll. *Jer.* xxxvi. 2.

Q. Are epistles or letters mentioned in Scripture?

A. Very rarely in the earliest ages.

Q. Where is the first one spoken of?

A. David wrote a letter to Joab, and sent it by the hand of Uriah. 2 *Sam.* xi. 14.

Q. Give another instance. 2 *Kings*, v. 6.*

A. The king of Syria sent a letter to the king of Israel, asking him to cure his servant Naaman of the leprosy.

Q. How were letters usually sent? *Nehem.* vi. 5.

A. Unsealed, except when sent to persons of high rank; then they were put in a valuable purse, closed with wax, and sealed with a signet. 1 *Kings*, xxi. 8.

Q. How did the most ancient epistles begin and end?

A. Without either salutation or farewell; and under the Persian monarchy they were very prolix.

Q. How were books written?

A. They were written on long rolls of parchment, which were rolled upon a stick or cylinder; the writing only on one side.

---

* 2 Kings, xix. 14; Ezra, iv. 7.

Lesson Twenty-third.

CARVING AND PAINTING.

Q. Did the Jews attain to much excellence in carving or sculpture?

A. No; though it was carried to some extent, as is evident from the cherubim which were placed in the Temple.

Q. Give another instance. 1 *Kings*, x. 20.

A. The twelve lions which were on each side of Solomon's throne.

Q. Give another from Isaiah, xliv. 13, 17.

A. Isaiah gives there the description of the manner in which idols were made.

Q. What was forbidden by the Mosaic law besides images? *Ex.* xx. 4.

A. The painting of pictures which were used for idolatrous purposes by the neighboring nations.

Q. Where is painting first spoken of in Scripture?

A. Jeremiah speaks of apartments which were painted with vermilion. *Jer.* xxii. 14.

Q. What does Ezekiel say of painting? *Ezek*, xxiii. 14.

A. He speaks of "men portrayed upon the wall, the images of the Chaldeans portrayed with vermilion."

Q. Whence were these pictures copied?

A. Probably from their heathen neighbors, after they had been corrupted by them.

Q. What were the Jews commanded to do in their wars with heathen nations? *Num.* xxxiii. 52.

A. They were commanded to "destroy all their pictures, and all their molten images."

Q. Do the books of Moses speak of the mechanic arts?

A. No express mention is made of them; and yet we early see signs of skill in the building of Noah's Ark and the Tower of Babel.

Q. Give another instance.

A. There was the use of balances in the time of Abraham; and chariots are spoken of in Genesis, xli. 43.

Q. Where did surveying take its origin?

A. In Egypt, whence the Jews brought it, and it enabled them to divide the land of Canaan.

Q. What do we find in the Book of Ezekiel, in reference to this subject? *Ez.* xl. 3, 5.

A. A line, or rope, for the purpose of taking measurements, is alluded to.

Q. Where are measures of length first spoken of?

A. God gave Noah the dimensions of the ark, the length three hundred cubits, the breadth fifty cubits, and the height thirty. *Gen.* vi. 15.

Q. Where do we find weights spoken of for weighing solid bodies?

A. Abraham "weighed to Ephron five hundred shekels of silver, current money," for the field of Machpelah. *Gen.* xxiii. 16.

Lesson Twenty-fourth.

AGRICULTURE AND COMMERCE.

Q. What was man's chief employment in the earliest ages of the world?

A. Agriculture and the keeping of flocks.

Q. What did Moses, in order to encourage agriculture?

A. He apportioned to every citizen a certain quantity of land, and gave him the right of transmitting it to his heirs.

Q. What sort of grain was raised by the Jews?

A. Wheat, barley, lentiles, rye, fitches, cummin, flax, and cotton. *Isa.* xxviii. 25.

Q. What fruits were abundant?

A. Grapes, figs, pomegranates, olives, and dates.*

Q. How was the soil cultivated at first?

A. At first with sharp sticks; afterwards it was loosened with shovels, and spades, and ploughs.

Q. How was grain reaped?

---

* Jahn's Archæology, p. 66.

A. It was reaped with a sickle.

Q. How was grain threshed?

A. At first it was beaten out with rods or sticks; afterwards it was trodden out by oxen.

Q. How was the grain prepared for use?

A. It was dried in the sun, and ground in hand-mills.

Q. What is said of the vineyards of the East?

A. Grapes grew spontaneously, in great quantities, and were also cultivated largely for wine.

COMMERCE.

Q. How was the commerce of the East carried on?

A. It was chiefly carried on by land; hence, ships are rarely mentioned.

Q. How did the people transport their goods?

A. By means of camels, and usually in large companies, called caravans. *Gen.* xxxvii. 25.

Q. What is the first direct notice of commerce in Scripture? 1 *Kings*, ix. 11.

A. David and Solomon carried on commerce with the Tyrians.

Q. What did they purchase of the king of Tyre?

A. Cedar and fir timber; large stones, cut and prepared for building; and gold.

Q. What did Solomon give in return? 1 *Kings*, v. 9, 11.

A. He furnished the Tyrians with corn, wine, and oil.

Q. Did the Jews build ships?

A. No; Tyrian carpenters were sent for, to build them at Ezion-geber, a port on the Red Sea. 1 *Kings*, ix. 26.

Q. With what other country did Solomon carry on trade? 1 *Kings*, x. 11, 28, 29.

A. With Egypt, whence he imported horses, carriages, and fine linen; and with Ophir, from which he obtained gold, silver, precious stones, and ivory.

Q. What may be said of the trading vessels of the Jews?

A. They were much inferior to those of modern times. They had no anchor or compass, and were dependent on the moon and stars for guidance.

Q. What sort of boat was used on the Nile?

A. A light boat, made of the reed papyrus.

Lesson Twenty-fifth.

MEASURES.

Q. How much was a finger? *Jer.* lii. 21.

A. It was three-quarters of an inch.

Q. What was a handbreadth? *Exod.* xxv. 25.

A. It was three inches and a half.

Q. What was a span? *Exod.* xxviii. 16.

A. It was three handbreadths, or ten and a half inches.

Q. What was a cubit? *Gen.* vi. 15.

A. It was two spans, or twenty-one inches.

Q. What was a fathom? *Acts*, xxvii. 28.

A. It was four cubits, which is seven feet three inches.

Q. What was a reed? *Ezek.* xl. 3, 5.

A. It was ten feet eleven inches.

Q. What was a line? *Ezek.* xl. 3.

A. It was eighty cubits, or one hundred and forty feet.

Q. What was a furlong? *Luke*, xxiv. 13.

A. Seven hundred feet, or two hundred and thirty-three yards.

Q. What was a mile?

A. It was eight furlongs.

Q. What was a Sabbath-day's journey?

A. Some authorities say one mile; others say two.

Q. What was a day's journey?

A. Thirty-three miles, one hundred and seventy-two paces, and four feet.

Q. What was an Eastern mile?

A. One English mile, four hundred and three paces, and one foot.

DRY MEASURES.

Q. What was a pot, or sextarius?
A. One and a half pints, English corn-measure.
Q. What was a cab? 2 *Kings*, vi. 25.
A. It was one quart, corn-measure.
Q. What was an omer, or tenth deal? *Exod.* xvi. 36.
A. It was two quarts and a pint.
Q. What was a seah?
A. It was one peck and one pint.
Q. What was an ephah? *Ezek.* xlv. 11.
A. Three pecks and three pints.
Q. What was a letech?
A. It was four bushels.
Q. What was a chomer, kor, or coros?
A. It was eight bushels.

LIQUID MEASURES.

Q. What was a log? *Lev.* xiv. 10.
A. About three-quarters of a pint.
Q. What was a cab?
A. It was three pints, wine-measure.
Q. What was a hin? *Exod.* xxix. 40.
A. It was five quarts.

Q. What was a seah?
A. It was ten quarts.
Q. What was a bath? 1 *Kings*, vii. 26.
A. Six hins, or seven gallons and two quarts.
Q. What was an homer? *Ezek.* xlv. 11.
A. It was seventy-five gallons.

Lesson Twenty-sixth.

COIN.

Q. What was the most ancient mode of carrying on trade?
A. It was carried on by barter or exchange.
Q. What was next received into traffic?
A. Such metals as were considered most valuable.
Q. How did they decide as to the value of the metal?
A. It was weighed out as it was needed, until the inconvenience of this mode led them to give to each metal a certain mark and value.
Q. When did the Jews first coin money?
A. In the reign of Judas Maccabeus, when Antiochus, king of Syria, granted them the privilege of coining their own money.
Q. What was the value of a gerah? *Exod.* xxx. 13.

A. It was about three cents, American money.

Q. What was a bekah? *Exod.* xxxviii. 26.

A. It was about thirty cents.

Q. What was a shekel of silver? *Exod.* xxx. 13.

A. It was fifty-six cents.

Q. What was a maneh, or mina, of silver?

A. It was about twenty-eight dollars.

Q. What was a talent of silver?

A. Seventeen hundred dollars.

Q. What was a shekel of gold worth?

A. It was worth nine dollars.

Q. What was a talent of gold?

A. Twenty-seven thousand three hundred and seventy-five dollars.

TAXES AND TRIBUTE.

Q. What was the first tax imposed upon the Jews? *Exod.* xxx. 13.

A. After the Tabernacle was built, there was a tax of half a shekel yearly levied on every male Israelite of twenty years of age and upwards.

Q. What tax was levied, after the return from the Babylonian captivity, for the temple service?

A. An annual payment of the third part of a shekel. *Nehem.* x. 32.

Q. Of whom did the Jews exact tribute, in the time of Joshua? *Josh.* xvi. 10; *Judges,* i. 28.

A. Of several of the Canaanitish tribes.

Q. Who paid tribute to David and Solomon?

A. The Moabites and Tyrians to David; and the Amorites, Hittites, Hivites, Perizzites, and Jebusites to Solomon.

Q. To whom did the Jews pay tribute in later times?

A. To the Persian kings; then to the Greeks, and finally to the Romans.

Q. Where did the tax-gatherers receive their taxes?

A. They placed themselves within the limits of the Temple, in the Gentiles' Court.

Q. What else do we find placed there?

A. Money-changers had their tables there also, and made a profit by exchanging money; these were overturned by the Lord Jesus.

Lesson Twenty-seventh.

DISEASES NAMED IN THE BIBLE.

Q. What diseases are mentioned in Scripture?

A. Leprosy, consumption, dropsy, lunacy, cancers, and pestilence.

Q. Which was the most formidable?

A. Leprosy, which was a skin disease, consisting of patches of white scales.

Q. What were the laws concerning leprosy?

A. Lepers were commanded to live apart by themselves, with the head bare, the chin covered, and garments rent, and were forbidden to touch any one.

Q. How long did the disease last without proving fatal?

A. One who had the disease from his birth might live fifty years.*

Q. What is the effect of the worst forms of this disease?

A. In time, it separates the joints and limbs, and mutilates the body in a shocking manner.

Q. What was the "pestilence" which is often mentioned in Scripture?

A. It was probably a species of plague, which was very rapid and fatal.

Q. What was the palsy that is named in the Bible?

A. It included several different maladies: apoplexy, catalepsy, and paralysis of a whole or part of the body.

Q. What is supposed to have been Nebuchadnezzar's disease?

---

* Jahn's Bib. Arch., p. 205.

A. It is supposed to have been hypochondriacal madness, and that he imagined himself an ox?

Q. What was the disease of Saul?

A. It was true madness, which returned at uncertain periods.

Q. What was Job's disease supposed to have been by some?

A. It was thought to have been small-pox by some persons; by others, to have been contagious leprosy.

Q. What disease of the mind is spoken of in the New Testament?

A. Demoniacal possession.

Q. What did that mean?

A. Evil spirits took possession of the mind and body of persons, and could not be exorcised, except by a miracle.

Q. What remedies were used by the Jews for diseases?

A. Very little is known of their remedies; external applications were much used.

Q. What remedy was much used in fevers?

A. Anointing with oil, which was very efficacious.

Q. What other remedy was much esteemed? *Jer.* viii. 22.

A. The balm of Gilead was celebrated.

Q. What was applied to wounds?

A. They were bound up with oil. *Luke* x. 34.

Q. Are physicians spoken of in Scripture?

A. Yes; Joseph had physicians to embalm the body of his father. *Gen.* l. 2; *Luke*, viii. 43.

Lesson Twenty-eighth.

TREATMENT OF THE DEAD.

Q. Was suicide common among the Jews?

A. No; instances of suicide are extremely rare: only three are recorded in Scripture.

Q. Give the instances.

A. Saul fell on his own sword; Ahithophel and Judas hanged themselves. 1 *Sam.* xxxi.; 2 *Sam.* xvii. 23; *Matt.* xxvii. 5.

Q. How did the Jews speak of death?

A. They compared it to a journey, a departure, or a sleep.

Q. What did they, as soon as life was extinct?

A. The eyes were closed by the nearest relative, who also gave a parting kiss to the body. *Gen.* xlvi. 4; l. i.

Q. What was done next?

A. The body was washed and laid out in an upper room.

Q. What was done to the bodies of persons of distinction?

A. They were embalmed with spices and aromatic drugs.

Q. How was this done?

A. The spices were put all around the body, and it was then bound tightly with linen bandages.

Q. What was often done at the burial of kings? 2 *Chron.* xvi. 14.

A. They "made a great burning," with spices, of the bed on which the deceased had lain, in order that no one else might have the honor of lying on it.

Q. What else did they burn?

A. They frequently burnt their armor, their clothing, and their bowels, with aromatic spices, as a sort of triumphant farewell to the deceased.

Q. What did the Jews to the body of King Saul and his sons? 1 *Sam.* xxxi. 12.

A. When they heard that Saul and his sons had been defeated by the Philistines, and were dead, they "brought their bodies, and burned them at Jabesh," and "buried their bones under a tree."

Q. In what other place is the burning of bodies mentioned?

A. The prophet Amos speaks of it; but it is evident from the words and from the context that it was in a time of pestilence, in which it was unsafe to go abroad to perform the funeral rites. *Amos*, vi. 10.

Q. What was denied to some persons, as a mark of great dishonor? *Eccles.* vi. 3.

A. The right of sepulture, or burial; and it was reckoned as one of the calamities which should befall the wicked.

Q. How did the Egyptians embalm bodies?

A. They made an incision in the side, took out the bowels, washed the body internally with palm wine, and then put a composition into it of myrrh, cassia, salt of nitre, etc.

Q. What was done with the head?

A. The brain was taken out through the nose with a crooked piece of iron, and the space filled with aromatic substances.

Q. What was then done?*

A. The body was wrapped tightly in linen and placed in a coffin of sycamore wood, and in this way was preserved in the house for ages, leaning against the wall.

Lesson Twenty-ninth.

FUNERALS OF THE JEWS.

Q. What was the Jewish custom, as to the time of burial?

A. Persons were buried soon after death.

---

* Jahn's Archæology, p. 237.

Q. Were coffins used by the Jews?*

A. No; the body was wrapped in folds of linen, with spices, and so placed in the tomb. *John*, xix. 40.

Q. How was it carried to interment?

A. Lying on an open couch, or bier, which is still the universal practice in Eastern countries.

Q. What does Josephus relate of King Herod's bier?

A. He says that "his body was carried on a golden bier, richly embroidered," to the tomb.†

Q. Who took charge of a funeral? *Gen.* xxiii. 19; xxv. 9.

A. The nearest relatives and friends of the deceased.

Q. What succeeded a funeral?

A. There was always a funeral feast after a burial.

Q. What signs of mourning did the family put on?

A. They rent their garments, and put on sackcloth and mourning apparel.

Q. What was customary in regard to mourners at a Jewish funeral?

A. Mourners were hired to weep and lament, and sing funeral dirges.

Q. What was customary at the funeral of a person of distinction? 2 *Sam.* iii. 33, 34.

A. A funeral oration, or poem, was pronounced: thus David made one over the grave of Abner.

---

* Jahn's Bib. Arch., p. 239.
† Joseph. Ant. Jud., lib. xvii. 8.

Q. What were buried with a warrior?

A. His weapons were laid by his side, and his sword put under his head. *Ezek.* xxxii. 27.

Q. What were the earliest sepulchres of which we have an account?

A. Caves. Abraham purchased the cave of Machpelah for a burial-place.

Q. Where were family sepulchres sometimes built?

A. Frequently in their gardens, near the house. *John*, xix. 41.

Q. What were the most simple monuments?

A. Hillocks of earth or heaps of stones on the grave.

Q. What was done in later times, to show respect for the dead?

A. Monuments were erected according to the means and rank of the family; the tombs of kings were very magnificent. *Isa.* xiv. 18.

Q. What monument was erected in honor of the family of the Maccabees at Modin?

A. A very high monument, built of square stones, with seven pyramids in front of it; and columns around it, with great stones placed on the tops, extending from one to the other.

Q. What were the Pyramids of Egypt?

A. They were built for the tombs of kings.*

---

* Jahn, Bib. Arch., p. 244.

PART II.

Lesson Thirtieth.

POLITICAL ANTIQUITIES.

Q. What was the first form of government of the Jews?

A. The Patriarchal.

Q. What was that?

A. The head or founder of the family exercised absolute power over his family, children, and servants.

Q. How far did they exercise this power?

A. They disinherited their children, and also punished them with death.

Q. Who were among the first patriarchs?

A. Abraham, Isaac, and Jacob.

Q. Who inherited the power on the death of the father?

A. The oldest son.

Q. Who were appointed to assist in the government, as the posterity of the patriarchs increased?

A. Magistrates, or governors, called Elders.

Q. What form of government was instituted by

Jehovah, on the departure of the Israelites from Egypt?

A. A new form of government called a Theocracy.

Q. What does Theocracy mean?

A. The people were governed by the immediate direction of God.

Q. How did God give laws to the Jews?

A. Through the mediation of his chosen servant Moses.

Q. How was God consulted in matters of great importance?

A. By Urim and Thummim.

Q. What were the Urim and Thummim?

A. An oracle worn on the breast of the high-priest, which indicated the will of God.

Q. How were questions answered by this oracle?

A. When the answer was in the affirmative, the jewels shone with great brilliancy, and became dull when a negative was intended.*

Q. In what other way did God make known his will?

A. By prophets, and by dreams and visions.

---

* There is great uncertainty about it. Some suppose it was a sacred lot; that there were three precious stones, on one of which was written *yes*, and on the other *no*, the third having no inscription; when no answer was to be returned, this was drawn.

Q. What was the chief principle of the Mosaic law?

A. The maintenance of the doctrine and worship of *one true God*, and the prevention of idolatry.

Q. Who were set apart by the Almighty to preserve and transmit true religion?

A. The posterity of Abraham, Isaac, and Jacob.

Q. What were the Jews taught to feel towards God?

A. The deepest reverence; and not only to worship Him as God, but to honor and obey Him as their King?

Q. How were they to regard the Tabernacle and Temple?

A. Not only as the Temple of Jehovah, but as the palace of their King.

Q. How did they regard the priests?

A. As the servants of God, who were bound to attend to secular as well as sacred affairs, and received tithes from the people as their salary.

Lesson Thirty-first.

JUDGES OF ISRAEL, AND KINGS.

Q. Who assisted Moses in the administration of the laws while the Israelites were in the Wilderness?

A. Moses established a council of seventy persons, skilled in the laws, to assist him.

Q. What other persons are spoken of in the Israelitish congregation?

A. Shoterim, or Scribes, who kept the genealogical tables, with a record of the births, deaths, and marriages.

Q. What did Moses order after their establishment in Canaan? *Deut.* xvi. 18.

A. That they should appoint judges and officers in every city.

Q. What was the term of office of a judge?

A. It was for life, in most cases.

Q. What was one of the most important duties of the judges?

A. They declared war, led armies, and concluded peace.

Q. How were judges treated?

A. With great respect and reverence, though they wore no outward badges of distinction.

Q. What privileges did they enjoy?

A. "They enjoyed no special privileges; they served their country without reward, that it might be prosperous, and that *God alone might be King in Israel.*"*

Q. What was the power of the judges?

A. It was equal to that of kings, and they decided causes absolutely.

---

* Jahn, p. 264.

Q. How were they supported?

A. They were supported solely by presents.

Q. How long did this form of government last?

A. About four hundred years, from Joshua to Saul.

Q. What change then took place?

A. The people desired a king, and God gave them one.

Q. Who was the first king?

A. Saul, the son of Kish.

Q. What was the power of the kings?

A. They were the viceroys of Jehovah, and their power was limited.

Q. How were kings inaugurated?

A. With great pomp, and with various ceremonies.

Q. What was the principal ceremony?

A. The king was anointed with holy anointing oil.

Q. What was done next?

A. A crown was placed upon his head, and a sceptre in his hand.

Q. What power had the king in the matter of his successor?

A. It was customary for the king to nominate his successor.

Q. Of what did his revenues consist?

A. Of voluntary offerings, or presents, and a tenth part of the produce of the fields and vineyards.

Q. What else do we learn of their income from 1 Kings, x. 14.

A. That the Israelites paid King Solomon a tax in money.

Lesson Thirty-second.

KINGS AND OFFICERS OF COURT.

Q. What was the government under the kings?

A. It was a limited monarchy.

Q. How was the power of the kings circumscribed?

A. By a code of fundamental and equal laws, provided by the Almighty.

Q. What were kings considered?

A. They were looked upon as reigning by Divine right.

Q. What right had the kings in the matter of war?

A. They could declare war and make peace, and also had the power of life and death, and of granting pardons to offenders.

Q. What else had they power to do? 1 *Sam.* xxii. 17, 18.*

A. They had the power to depose or condemn to

---

* Horne's Introduction, vol. ii., p. 43.

death even the high-priest and priests. 1 *Kings*, ii. 26, 27.

Q. What other ecclesiastical right had the king?

A. He had the power to reform gross abuses in religion.

Q. Was the government under the kings similar to that of the judges?

A. Yes; with but one difference.

Q. What was that?

A. The conduct of the judges was regulated by Urim and Thummim; that of the kings, by inspiration of God, or by prophets raised up to reclaim them, when departing from their duty.

Q. What oath did the king take?

A. He took an oath that he would govern according to the law of Moses; and to a covenant which defined the principles for the conduct of the government.

Q. Who was the most important officer at the royal court? 2 *Chron.* xxviii. 7.

A. The prime minister, or "next to the king," as he is called in Scripture.

Q. Give examples.

A. Joseph was prime minister to Pharaoh; Jonathan to David; Haman to Ahasuerus.

Q. Who were next the prime minister?*

A. The royal counsellors, or privy council.

---

* Horne's Introd., vol. ii., p. 46.

Q. What other persons held a high place at court as advisers of the king?

A. The prophets, who were always consulted by the pious kings. 2 *Sam.* viii. 2.

Q. What other important officer is mentioned?

A. The recorder, whose duty it was to keep a daily register of every thing that occurred at court. 2 *Sam.* viii. 6.

Q. Who else was reckoned among the royal counsellors.

A. The high-priest.

Q. What were the duties of the scribe?

A. The scribe was the king's secretary of state, who issued the royal commands.

Q. How were the laws proclaimed to the people?

A. They were publicly proclaimed by criers.

Q. How were edicts made known to distant provinces?

A. By couriers, specially sent for the purpose.

Q. What were Cherethites? 2 *Sam.* xx. 23.

A. They were the king's life-guard; and also executed sentence of death when it had been pronounced by the king. 1 *Kings* ii. 25.

Lesson Thirty-third.

KINGS CONTINUED.

Q. How long did the twelve tribes remain united under one king?

A. For one hundred and twenty years.

Q. How many kings had they during this period?

A. Three; Saul, David, and Solomon.

Q. What happened at the death of Solomon?

A. The kingdom was divided by the revolt of the ten tribes.

Q. What were they then called?

A. The kingdoms of Israel and Judah.

Q. What were the inhabitants called?

A. Israelites and Jews.

Q. What name had been previously given to the nation? *Gen.* xiv. 13.

A. Hebrews, from "Abram the Hebrew," who was the founder of the nation.

Q. How long did the kingdom of Israel continue?

A. It continued under various kings for a period of two hundred and fifty-four years.

Q. What happened at the end of that time?

A. The ten tribes were conquered and taken captives by Shalmaneser, king of Assyria. 2 *Kings*, xvii. 6.

Q. How long did the kingdom of Judah last?

A. About three hundred and eighty-eight years,

when it was conquered by the Chaldeans, under Nebuchadnezzar. 2 *Kings*, xxv. 1, 21.

Q. What did Nebuchadnezzar with the inhabitants?

A. He carried them captive to Babylon, where they remained seventy years. B. C. 588.

Q. How many kings had Judah during this period of three hundred and eighty-eight years?

A. Twenty kings.

Q. How many kings had Israel?

A. Eighteen.

Q. What was the capital of Judah?

A. Jerusalem.

Q. What was the capital of Israel?

A. Samaria.

Q. Where did the Jews worship?

A. In Solomon's Temple, at Jerusalem.

Q. Where did the Israelites worship?

A. At the temple which they built on Mount Gerizim.

Q. What was the state of religion among the Jews?

A. Pure religion was much more carefully preserved among them than with the Israelites.

Q. What prevailed extensively among the Israelites?

A. The vilest idolatry was common among them.

Q. What was the general character of the kings of Judah?

A. They were much more exemplary than the kings of Israel; and the kingdom continued for many years in peaceable subjection to its lawful sovereigns.

Q. What was one probable cause of this?

A. Their attachment was so strong to the family of David, that nothing could lessen their fidelity to the royal lineage.

Q. Who was to come from the tribe of Judah, and family of David?

A. Christ the Saviour was to be born of this line, and they were aware of this fact.

Lesson Thirty-fourth.

KINGS OF ISRAEL AND JUDAH.

Q. What was the general condition of the people of the kingdom of Israel?

A. They were distracted by civil wars, seditions, and the contests of ambitious aspirants to the throne.

Q. What was the final result of these contests?

A. They were divided, provinces revolted, and they became an easy conquest to the king of Assyria.

Q. What became of the Israelites?

A. The rich were carried captive beyond the Euphrates, but the poorer classes remained in their own country.

Q. What was the state of religion among them?

A. Idolatry was practised among the Israelites, probably from their intermarriage with the heathen nations, by whom they were surrounded.

Q. What idol was worshipped at Samaria?

A. Baal; and this was one great cause of the bitter hatred existing between the Jews and Samaritans.

Q. What was the character of the kings of Israel?

A. They governed so ill as scarcely to deserve the name of sovereigns.*

Q. What do the sacred historians record of them?

A. That they departed not from all the sins of Jeroboam, the son of Nebat, who made Israel to sin. 2 *Kings*, x. 29.

Q. What was the condition of the tribes of Judah who were carried captive to Babylon?†

A. They were probably viewed as colonists, and some of them were treated with much kindness and distinction.

Q. From what is this manifest? *Dan.* ii. 48.

A. From the fact that the Prophet Daniel held the first office at the court of the king of Assyria.

Q. Give another instance. *Dan.* iii. 12.

A. Daniel's three friends, Shadrach, Meshach, and Abednego, also occupied important stations at court.

Q. Give another instance. 2 *Kings*, xxv. 27.

---

* Horne's Introduction, vol. ii., p. 49. † Ib. 50.

A. Jehoiachim, the king of Judah, ate at the table of his conqueror, and received an annual allowance corresponding to his rank. 2 *Kings*, xxv. 30.

Q. When were the Jews released from their captivity?

A. When Cyrus, king of Persia, took Babylon, he permitted the Jews to return to Jerusalem.

Q. What permission did Cyrus give the Jews?

A. He authorized them to rebuild the temple, and to enjoy their own religion and laws. *Ezra* i. 1, 3.

Q. What did Cyrus restore to the Jews?

A. All the vessels of gold and silver belonging to the temple which Nebuchadnezzar had taken from it.

Q. What form of government was then resumed?

A. The Theocratic government was restored.

Q. How was the rebuilding of the temple accomplished?

A. It was effected by two divinely inspired governors, Ezra and Nehemiah. B. C. 543.

Q. How were the Jews governed after the death of of Ezra and Nehemiah?

A. By high-priests, in subjection to the Persian kings.

Lesson Thirty-fifth.

KINGS OF JUDAH.

Q. How long did the kingdom of Judah continue in subjection to foreign power?

A. For about three hundred years.

Q. What happened then?

A. Antiochus Epiphanes, king of Syria, cruelly oppressed them, and they were forced to take up arms in their own defence.

Q. How did the Jews succeed in this war for independence?

A. They maintained a religious war for twenty-six years, under Judas Maccabeus and his brothers, and finally established their independence.

Q. How long did the family of the Maccabees govern the Jews?

A. For a period of one hundred and twenty-six years.

Q. What happened about fifty-nine years before Christ?

A. The Romans, under Pompey, captured Jerusalem, and reduced it to a dependent province.*

Q. Who defeated Pompey, and again changed the government of the Jews?†

A. Julius Cæsar, who bestowed the government of

---

* Horne's Introd., vol. ii., p. 50. † Ib.

the Jews upon Antipater, an Idumean by birth, but of the Jewish religion; he was also the father of Herod the Great.

Q. What did Antipater with Judea?

A. He divided it into two parts, and gave the province of Galilee to his son Herod, and Jerusalem to Phasael.

Q. What title was bestowed on Herod by Mark Antony?

A. The title of King of Judea.

Q. How is Herod described by Josephus?

A. As a person of great resolution and courage, liberal in his expenditures, but cruel and passionate.

Q. Of what terrible crime was he guilty in regard to his own family?

A. He caused his wife and several children to be beheaded, and other members of his family also.

Q. What did Herod, in order to please the Jews?

A. He rebuilt the temple at Jerusalem, which had become much decayed, and spared no expense in making it as beautiful as possible.

Q. What great event occurred during the latter part of the reign of this wicked king?

A. The Saviour was born at Bethlehem; and the fear that Christ might become king of the Jews caused Herod to command that all the male children of Bethlehem should be put to death.

Q. Who was king of the Jews during the life of Christ?

A. Herod Antipas, son of Herod the Great.

Q. What did Judea then become?

A. It was fully recognized as a Roman province, and the "sceptre departed from Judah."

Q. What prophecy was thus fulfilled? *Gen.* xlix. 10.

A. The sceptre shall not depart from Judah ... until Shiloh come.

Q. When were the Jewish temple and state finally destroyed?

A. In the year of our Lord 70, by the Romans, under Titus.

Lesson Thirty-sixth.

JEWISH COURTS OF JUSTICE.

Q. Where did the Jews hold their courts of justice?

A. "The gate of the city" was the seat of justice. *Amos* v. 12; *Zech.* viii. 16.

Q. Who presided at these courts? *Deut.* xvi. 18.

A. Judges and officers were appointed to be in all their gates throughout their tribes.

Q. Where did the Jews hold their courts in the time of Christ? *Matt.* x. 17.

A. In their synagogues, where they punished the victim with scourging.

Q. Was there a higher court to which they could appeal?

A. Yes; weighty causes were carried before the supreme judge of the commonwealth, or before the high-priest. *Deut.* xvii. 8, 9.

Q. What do we find in regard to a supreme court at Jerusalem? 2 *Chron.* xix. 8.

A. Jehoshaphat, the king, established a court of priests and Levites, and chief fathers of Israel, to decide important causes.

Q. What was established in the time of the Maccabees?

A. A supreme judicial tribunal, called the Sanhedrim.

Q. Of whom was the Sanhedrim composed?

A. Of seventy members, under the presidency of the high-priest.

Q. What other officers were there?

A. Two vice presidents, the chief priests, elders, and scribes.

Q. Where did the Sanhedrim hold its sittings?

A. The Talmudists say, in the temple; but Josephus says they had a council-house in the vicinity of the Temple.

Q. At what other place were they sometimes held?

A. At the high-priest's house, as in the trial of our Saviour. *Luke* xxiv. 54.

Q. What were the preliminaries of a trial?

A. The accuser and accused both made their appearance before the judge and two secretaries.

Q. How many judges were present at a trial?

A. Josephus says that there was a tribunal of seven judges in every city.

Q. What other tribunal do the Talmudists speak of?*

A. A tribunal of twenty-three judges, which tried causes of a religious nature.

Q. How many witnesses were required in order to establish a charge?

A. Two or three witnesses were required in a matter of life and death. *Deut.* xvii. 6.

Q. How was sentence of death pronounced?

A. "He is guilty of death." *Matt.* xxvi. 66.

Q. What other way of pronouncing sentence was common in early times?

A. A person's condemnation was announced to him by giving him a black stone; and his acquittal, by giving him a white stone.

Q. Where do you find an allusion to this in the New Testament? *Rev.* ii. 17.

---

* Jahn, Arch., p. 303.

A. "To him that overcometh" will I "give a white stone."

Lesson Thirty-seventh.

TRIALS.

Q. At what time of day were courts held and criminals tried?

A. In the morning; and it was unlawful to try capital cases in the night.

Q. What was also forbidden by the law?

A. It was forbidden to try a cause, pass sentence, and execute the sentence in the same day.*

Q. On what occasion were all these laws broken?

A. In the trial of our Saviour, who was tried, condemned, and crucified at once. *Matt.* xxvi. 57, 66.

Q. Were witnesses sworn before testifying?

A. Yes; and in capital cases, the accused also. *Matt.* xxvi. 63.

Q. How were the witnesses examined?

A. They were examined separately; but the accused had the right to be present when they gave their testimony.

Q. When was sentence executed?

A. Immediately after it was pronounced.

---

* Jahn, Arch., p. 304.

Q. Could the king recall the sentence of death?

A. No; not when once passed.

Q. Was there a public executioner?

A. No; not in the early periods of Jewish history. When the punishment was stoning, the witnesses cast the first stone; then the people joined in the work. *Deut.* xvii. 7.

Q. Who executed sentence of death in later times?

A. When sentence of death was pronounced by the king, it was executed by his body-guard.

Q. Who sometimes executed the sentence? 1 *Sam.* xv. 33.

A. Persons of high rank; as, for instance, "Samuel," the Judge of Israel, " hewed Agag in pieces before the Lord."

Q. What was given to the condemned before execution?

A. Wine, with incense in it, to stupefy them.

Q. What was placed first on the list of crimes among the Jews?

A. Idolatry—that is, the worship of false gods.

Q. What was idolatry considered?

A. A crime against God, and also against the laws of the State, and, therefore, high treason.

Q. How was idolatry punished?

A. By stoning the guilty person to death.

Q. What command was given concerning a city which was guilty of idolatry? *Deut.* xiii. 15, 16.

A. God commanded that the people should be put to death, and the city burned with fire.

Q. Was this law often enforced?

A. No; because idolatry was so common.

Q. How then did God punish those cities?

A. By wars, pestilence, famine, and other national judgments.

Q. What other crimes were punished with death?

A. Murder, blasphemy, false prophesying, divination or magic, and perjury.

Lesson Thirty-eighth.

PUNISHMENTS.

Q. Where are prisons spoken of in Scripture?

A. Joseph and the butler and baker of Pharaoh were put in prison. *Gen.* xl. 3.

Q. To what were criminals subjected in prison?

A. They were liable to be confined with chains. *Jer.* xl. 4.

Q. What was the punishment of a debtor?

A. He was imprisoned, and sometimes punished with stripes. *Matt.* v. 26; xviii. 28, 34.

Q. What punishment is mentioned in Job, xiii. 27?

A. That of putting the feet in the stocks; and it was probably of Egyptian origin.

Q. What was the custom of the Jews in case of accidental murder or manslaughter? *Num.* xxxv. 26, 27.

A. The nearest relative of the murdered man had the right to kill the murderer wherever he found him.

Q. What provision was made for the protection of such persons?

A. Six cities of refuge were appointed, into which the homicide might flee, and there remain in safety until he could be tried by the congregation.

Q. What might happen, if he was found without the city walls?

A. The "revenger of blood" might kill him on the spot.

Q. How long was the homicide to remain in the city of refuge?

A. "Until the death of the high-priest," when he could return to his home in safety. *Num.* xxxv. 28.

Q. What was the punishment for stealing?

A. Moses imposed the punishment of double restitution.

Q. What was done if the thief had nothing with which to make restitution?

A. He was sold as a slave, and payment was made out of the purchase-money.

Q. What were some of the modes of punishment among the Jews?

A. Stoning, beheading, hanging, slaying with a sword, pounding in a mortar, and sawing asunder.

Q. What cruel mode of executing a criminal was introduced into Judea by the Romans?

A. Crucifixion, which was inflicted only on the greatest criminals.

Q. How was it done?

A. A cross was made of two beams of wood, and the hands and feet of the victim were nailed or tied to it.

Q. What indignities were offered the victim?

A. He was scourged with whips, pricked with goads, spit upon, and compelled to bear the cross to the place of execution.

Q. What was sometimes done after the crucifixion?

A. The legs of the sufferer were sometimes broken. *John,* xix. 31, 32.

Q. How long did persons live on the cross?

A. Sometimes two or three days.

Lesson Thirty-ninth.

MILITARY ANTIQUITIES.

Q. What account have we in Scripture of military affairs?

A. Very little information is given on this subject.

Q. What was the first battle of which we have any account?

A. That of Abram and his trained servants, who delivered his brother Lot from Chedorlaomer. *Gen.* xiv. 17.

Q. At what age were the Jews liable to military service?

A. From twenty to fifty years of age. *Num.* i. 3.

Q. How were troops levied? *Num.* xxxi. 4, 5.

A. If the case was urgent, all were summoned to war; but if not, a certain number were selected from each tribe.

Q. How were they supported? 1 *Sam.* xvii. 13, 17.

A. Every one served at his own expense, and generally carried his own arms and provisions.

Q. What is the first record of a standing army in time of peace? 1 *Sam.* xiii. 1, 2.

A. During the reign of Saul, a small military force was retained.

Q. Did the Jewish armies ever become numerous? 2 *Chron.* xiv. 8, 9.

A. Yes; Asa, king of Judah, had an army of nearly six hundred thousand men, with which he defeated Zerah, the Ethiopian, who had an army of one million of men.

Q. How was the army divided?

A. Into three bands or divisions, corresponding with the division of modern times—the centre, left and right wings

Q. Who was the first and principal head of the armies of Israel? 2 *Sam.* vi. 2.

A. The Almighty, who is often called in Scripture, the Lord of Hosts.

Q. Who was the lieutenant-general of the Jewish army?

A. The commander-in-chief was called the "Captain of the Lord's host."

Q. What were the other officers called?

A. Captains of thousands, captains of hundreds, captains of fifties.

Q. Did kings ever go to war in person?

A. Yes; and fought on foot, like their soldiers.

Q. What attendants had they?

A. They had armor-bearers, who were chosen from the bravest of the soldiers.

Q. What was their duty?

A. They were employed to give orders to the captains, to bear the arms of their master, and to be at his side in the hour of peril. 1 *Sam.* xiv. 6; xvii. 7.

Q. How were officers appointed?

A. Some of them were appointed by the king, and

in other instances the office was permanent and hereditary in the heads of families.*

Lesson Fortieth.

ARMIES OF THE JEWS.

Q. Had the Jews any cavalry in their armies?

A. There is no account of any until the time of Solomon. 1 *Kings*, x. 28, 29.

Q. Where did Solomon procure horses? 1 *Kings*, x. 29.

A. He got them from Egypt, at great expense.

Q. What was the price of a horse?

A. One hundred and fifty shekels of silver, which was nearly one hundred dollars.

Q. How did kings sometimes go into battle?

A. In chariots; sometimes in their royal vestments, and sometimes in disguise. 1 *Kings*, xxii. 30, 35.

Q. What were much used in war, among the Israelites as well as the Egyptians?

A. War chariots made of iron, with scythes fastened to the wheels. 2 *Mac.* xiii. 2.

---

* Jahn's Arch., p. 333.

Q. Where are they first mentioned in the Bible? *Ex.* xiv. 7.

A. The most ancient were those of Pharaoh, which were destroyed in the Red Sea.

Q. What engines of war were erected by King Uzziah upon the towers of the walls of the city?

A. They were of two kinds: Catapults and balistæ.

Q. What were catapults?*

A. They were immense bows, which were bent by a machine, and threw with great force arrows, javelins, and even beams of wood.

Q. What were the balistæ?

A. They were large slings, which were discharged by machines, and threw stones, and balls of lead.

Q. What other instrument of war is mentioned by Ezekiel? *Ezek.* iv. 2.

A. The battering-ram: which was a long, stout beam of oak, the ends of which were brass.

Q. How was it used?

A. It was carried on the arms of the soldiers, and impelled against the wall.

Q. What arms were most anciently used? *Ps.* ii. 9; *Prov.* xxv. 18.

A. The arms used in fighting hand to hand were a club, a battle-hammer of iron, and a sword.

---

* Jahn's Arch., p. 343.

Q. How were the infantry armed?

A. The light-armed troops had a sling, a javelin, bow, arrows, and quiver, and fought the enemy at a distance.

Q. What was the sling?

A. It is reckoned as among the most ancient instruments of warfare, and threw a stone from a string or rope.

Q. What were arrows made of?

A. They were made of wood, with an iron point, which was sometimes poisoned.

Q. What was also common?

A. A shrub called the broom was put on the end of the arrow, set on fire, and then discharged.*

Q. What reference is made to this fact in Zech. ix. 14?

A. "His arrow shall be sent forth as the lightning."

Lesson Forty-first.

ARMIES—CONTINUED.

Q. How were the spearmen armed?

A. They had spears, swords, shields, and battle-axes, and fought hand to hand.

---

* Jahn's Arch., p. 342.

Q. What were the defensive arms of the Hebrews?

A. The helmet, breastplate, shield, military girdle, and boots or greaves.

Q. What was the helmet?

A. It was a covering for the head, made of brass.

Q. What was the breastplate?

A. A covering for the breast, made of brass or iron.

Q. Of what was the shield made? 1 *Kings*, x. 17.

A. It was made of wood, and covered with brass or gold.

Q. What were greaves? 1 *Sam.* xvii. 6.

A. They were large boots, sometimes covered with plates of brass.

Q. What did the Jews consult before a battle?

A. They consulted the Urim and Thummim, which glowed with great brilliancy if they were to be victorious. They also consulted the prophets of the Lord.

Q. How were the wars of the Jews carried on?

A. With great cruelty and ferocity.

Q. Give an instance.

A. On one occasion, ten thousand prisoners of war were taken out and cast from the top of a rock, which killed them all.

Q. What other indignities were often inflicted on captives?

A. The victors set their feet upon their necks, and mutilated their persons. *Josh.* x. 24; *Judges*, i. 7.

Q. Quote the latter text from Judges.

A. Adoni-bezek said: "Threescore and ten kings, having their thumbs and great toes cut off, gathered their meat under my table."

Q. How were victors received on their return home?

A. They were met by women, who preceded them with instruments of music, singing, and dancing. *Ex.* xv. 20, 21.

Q. What was done with the spoils of war? *Num.* xxxi. 54.

A. A portion of the gold was taken into the Tabernacle, for a memorial unto the Lord.

Q. How much did the king receive? *Gen.* xiv. 20.

A. The king had a tenth of what was taken.*

Q. If any article of great value was found among the spoil, what was done with it? 2 *Sam.* xii. 30.

A. It was at once given to the commander-in-chief.

Q. What was done with the remainder of the spoil?

A. It was divided into two parts: half was given to the soldiers, and half to those who remained at

---

* Jahn's Arch., p. 371.

home, but who would have gone, if necessary, to the war. *Num.* xxxi. 27; 1 *Sam.* xxx. 24.

Q. What did they with part of the spoil in the time of the Maccabees? 2 *Mac.* viii. 28.

A. They gave part of the spoils to the maimed, and to the widows and orphans, and divided the rest among themselves.

Q. On what occasion were all the silver and gold devoted to God for the Temple?

A. When the city of Jericho was taken on the Sabbath-day.

PART III.

Lesson Forty-second.

SACRED ANTIQUITIES.

Q. Where did the patriarchs worship God?

A. They worshipped in groves and on mountains, where they erected altars, on which to offer sacrifice.

Q. What did Noah when he came out of the ark?

A. He built an altar, and offered sacrifice to God.

Q. What did Abraham?

A. He built altars wherever he pitched his tent.

Q. Where did Jacob worship? *Gen.* xxviii. 18, 22.

A. He set up stones for a pillar, poured oil upon it, and called it "God's house."

Q. In what did the worship of God consist at that early period?

A. "Chiefly of tithes, vows, prayers, and sacrifices."*

Q. What portion of time did God command them to keep holy? *Gen.* ii. 2.

A. One day in seven, called the Sabbath, which means rest.

Q. Where did the Jews worship during their sojourn in the Wilderness?

A. At the Tabernacle, which was the place of their most solemn public worship.

Q. By whom was the Tabernacle built?

A. By Moses, under the direction of the Almighty.

Q. What was the form of the Tabernacle?

A. It was in the form of a tent, which could easily be removed from one place to another.

---

* Jahn's Archæology, p. 380.

Q. Where was the Tabernacle first set up?

A. In the wilderness of Sinai; and it was carried from place to place, as the Israelites journeyed to the land of Canaan.

Q. What materials were used in building the Tabernacle? *Exod.* xxv.

A. Gold, silver, brass, fragrant wood, curtains of blue, purple, and scarlet, and other costly materials.

Q. What things were placed in the Tabernacle?

A. The Ark of the Covenant, the cherubim, the altar for incense, a table for the shew-bread, and the golden candlestick.

Q. What was the Ark of the Covenant?

A. A small chest, made of wood, overlaid with gold.

Q. What was kept in the Ark?

A. The tables of stone, containing the Ten Commandments, the pot of manna, and Aaron's rod.

Q. What was the lid or covering of the ark?

A. It was made of solid gold, and was called the Mercy-seat.

Q. What rested on this Mercy-seat? *Lev.* xvi. 2.

A. The Shekinah, or Divine Presence, rested upon it, in the form of a cloud.

Q. How were the Divine commands given from this place?

A. In an audible voice, as often as Jehovah was consulted on behalf of His people.

Lesson Forty-third.

SOLOMON'S TEMPLE.

Q. Where was the first temple built for the worship of God, and by whom?

A. On the summit of Mount Moriah, by Solomon, the third king of Israel.

Q. How long was this Temple in building?

A. Seven years.

Q. What is said of this Temple by Jewish writers?

A. They say it was more beautiful than any thing ever before erected by man.

Q. Of what was the Temple built?

A. Of the purest white marble, gold, silver, brass, cedar-wood, and precious stones in abundance.

Q. What was the place called the Holy of Holies?

A. It was the innermost central part, also called the sanctuary.

Q. What was the area called which immediately surrounded the Holy of Holies and the altar?

A. It was called the "court of the priests," and it was surrounded by a low inclosure, so that the people could look into it, but could not enter.

Q. By what was this inclosure surrounded?

A. By two other courts; the inner one for the

Jews to worship in, the outer court for the Gentiles, who were forbidden to approach nearer.

Q. What was placed in the sanctuary?

A. The Ark of the Covenant, which was concealed from view by a costly Babylonian veil.

Q. Of what was the altar made on which sacrifices were offered?

A. It was made of unhewn stones, covered with brass.

Q. Where was the altar of incense placed?

A. It was within the sanctuary, and was covered with gold.

Q. What was always kept burning on this altar?

A. The sacred fire; and incense was burned upon it at the morning and evening sacrifice.

Q. When was this Temple built?

A. One thousand years before Christ.

Q. How long did it retain its splendor?

A. Only thirty-three years, when it was plundered by Shishak, king of Egypt.

Q. When was it entirely destroyed?

A. It was burned by the Chaldeans, under Nebuchadnezzar, 584 years before Christ.

Q. By whom was the second Temple built?

A. By the Jews, after their return from the captivity in Babylon.

Q. Who gave them permission to return to Judea?

A. Cyrus, king of Persia, conquered Babylon, and

permitted the Jews to return and rebuild their Temple. B. C. 535.

Q. How did the Jews obtain the means to rebuild the Temple?

A. The annual tax of a half shekel from every Jew, wherever he might be, and presents from proselytes, gave them an immense amount of treasure.

Lesson Forty-fourth.

TEMPLE—CONTINUED.

Q. What was lacking in this second Temple?

A. The Ark of the Covenant, the sacred oil, the sacred fire, and the Shekinah.

Q. What was the Shekinah?

A. It was the visible presence of Jehovah, in the form of a cloud, which rested on the Mercy-seat.

Q. What was the size of this Temple?

A. It was larger than Solomon's Temple, but not nearly so beautiful.

Q. When was it plundered and profaned?

A. B. C. 163, by Antiochus Epiphanes, who offered swine's flesh on the altar, "which was an abomination to the Lord."

Q. What did Antiochus place upon the altar?

A. He placed a statue of Jupiter Olympus on the altar.

Q. How long did it continue there? *2 Mac.* x. 1, 8, 9.

A. Three years, when Judas Maccabeus repaired and purified the temple, and restored the true worship of God.

Q. What happened to this Temple in course of time?

A. It became decayed, and needed repairs.

Q. Who undertook to rebuild it?

A. Herod the Great, son of Antipater.

Q. How many men did he employ upon it?

A. He "employed eighteen thousand men for nine years upon it, and spared no expense in order to make it superior to any thing known among mankind."*

Q. What did the Jews continue to do?

A. They constantly made additions, expending a vast amount of treasure, so that they really were "forty and six years in building."

Q. When was it completed?

A. Only a short time before our Saviour began his ministry.

Q. What does Josephus say of this Temple?

A. He says: "The inner Temple, or sanctuary,

---

* Horne's Introd., vol. ii., p. 98.

was covered on every side with plates of gold; so that, when the sun shone upon it, the eye could not bear the dazzling light of its radiance."

Q. In what respect did the second Temple surpass the first?

A. By being honored with the frequent bodily presence of our Saviour, according to the prophecy of Haggai (ii. 9).

Q. What did Christ prophesy of this Temple?

A. "That not one stone should be left upon another that should not be thrown down."

Q. When was this prophecy fulfilled?

A. This Temple was destroyed by the Romans, under Titus, thirty-seven years after the death of Christ.

Q. What other temples were erected?

A. Two others; one in the city of Leontopolis, in Egypt, by Onias, the high-priest; the other on Mount Gerizim, by Sanballat, for the Samaritans.

Lesson Forty-fifth.

SYNAGOGUES.

Q. What were synagogues?
A. They were the parish churches of the Jews.
Q. What services were held in the synagogues?

A. The people assembled there for prayer, reading, hearing, and expounding the Scriptures.

Q. When is it supposed they were first introduced into Judea?

A. During the reign of the Asmonean princes.*

Q. How were synagogues built?

A. They were built in imitation of the Temple at Jerusalem, with a court and porches.

Q. What were the uppermost seats in the synagogue? †

A. Those nearest the altar, which were esteemed peculiarly honorable. *Matt.* xxiii. 6.

Q. Who had charge of the synagogue?

A. There were three officers who had charge.

Q. What was the first officer called? *Luke*, xiii. 14.

A. The ruler of the synagogue.

Q. What was his duty?

A. He regulated all its concerns, and gave permission to persons to preach.

Q. What other name was given to these rulers?

A. That of sages, or wise men.‡

Q. What powers had they? *Matt.* x. 17.

A. They were judges of thefts and other small offences, and had the power of inflicting punishments.

---

* Jahn, Bib. Arch., p. 486.   † Horne, vol. ii., p. 104.   ‡ Ib.

Q. What was the second officer called?

A. The angel of the church.

Q. What was his duty?

A. To offer public prayer to God for the whole congregation.

Q. Why was he called angel?

A. Because, as their messenger, he spoke to God for them.

Q. What was the third officer?

A. The chazan, or minister, whose duty it was to take charge of the sacred books.

Q. What is said of the prayers of the Jews?

A. They had liturgies, in which were all the prescribed forms of the synagogue worship.

Q. What does the ancient Samaritan chronicle say of these liturgics?

A. The Jews had a book of prayers which they used in their public services from the time of Moses.

Q. What did these books contain?*

A. "Services for the Passover, the marriage, the burial, for times of sorrow and joy, and the Psalms of David."

Q. For what other purpose was the synagogue used?

A. Their children were taught in the synagogues by the sages.

---

* Sinclair's Dissertations, p. 10.

JEWISH ANTIQUITIES. 115

Q. What other places, built purposely for prayer, are mentioned in Jewish histories?

A. The proseuchæ, or oratories, which were built outside the city walls, on the banks of rivers, or on the seashore, in order that people who lived at a distance from the Temple might offer their prayers in them.*

Lesson Forty-sixth.

SACRED SEASONS.

Q. What was the first festival or holy-day?

A. The Sabbath; which was instituted by God to preserve the memory of the creation of the world.

Q. What did Moses institute to perpetuate the memory of the wonders God had wrought for the Jews?

A. He instituted various festivals, which they were bound to observe.

Q. What day of the week was the Sabbath of the Jews?

A. The seventh day, or Saturday.

Q. How were they commanded to keep the Sabbath?

---

* Horne's Introd., vol. ii., p. 102.

A. They were commanded to keep it holy, and to have a holy convocation every seventh day.

Q. What punishment was denounced for the wilful profanation of the Sabbath?

A. The punishment was death.

Q. Quote an instance where this was carried out. *Num.* xv. 32–36.

A. They found a man gathering sticks on the Sabbath-day, and the congregation stoned him to death.

Q. When did the Sabbath commence?

A. It commenced at sunset, and closed at sunset on the following day. *Matt.* viii. 16.*

Q. What was permitted on the Sabbath?

A. The Jews had feasts on the Sabbath-day; but every thing was prepared on the previous day.

Q. What were the other five great festivals?

A. The Passover, the day of Pentecost, the Feast of Tabernacles, the Feast of Trumpets, and the Great Day of Expiation.

Q. What did the Feast of the Passover commemorate?

A. The departure of the Israelites from Egypt.

Q. When was it instituted?

A. On the night before they left Egypt.

Q. Why was it so called?

---

* Horne's Introd., vol. ii., p. 122.

A. Because the angel of death *passed over* the houses of the Israelites, when he slew the children of the Egyptians.

Q. When was the Passover kept?

A. On the fourteenth day of the month Nisan, and it continued seven days.

Q. With what does this correspond?

A. With the latter part of the month of March.

Q. How was the Feast of the Passover celebrated?

A. A lamb of the first year was sacrificed, the blood sprinkled upon the altar, and the fat consumed on the altar.

Q. What was then done?

A. The lamb was roasted whole, and eaten with bitter herbs and unleavened bread.

Q. What number of persons constituted a Paschal society?

A. About ten persons to one lamb.

Q. What was done at the conclusion of the supper?

A. The person officiating took bread and wine and blessed it, and gave it to all who were present.

Q. What was done last of all?

A. They sang the great Hallel, or hymn of praise; (Psalms 115, 116, 117, 118.)

Lesson Forty-seventh.

THE FEAST OF PENTECOST.

Q. What was the second great festival?

A. The Feast of Pentecost.

Q. Why was it so called?

A. Because it was celebrated fifty days after the first day of the Passover.

Q. By what other names was it called?

A. The feast of weeks, the feast of harvest, and the day of first-fruits. *Ex.* xxxiv. 22; *Ex.* xxiii. 16: *Num.* xviii. 12.

Q. For what did they thank God at this festival?

A. They offered thanksgivings to God for the bounties of the harvest.

Q. What else was commemorated on this day?

A. The giving of the law on Mount Sinai.

Q. What was the third of the great festivals?

A. The Feast of Tabernacles, celebrated on the fifteenth of Tisri.

Q. Why was it instituted?

A. To commemorate the dwelling of the Israelites in tents, while they wandered in the wilderness.

Q. What were they obliged to do during the whole of this feast?

A. They were obliged to dwell in tents during the seven weeks in which the feast continued.

Q. What was done on the last day of this feast?

A. The Jews brought water from the Pool of Siloam in a golden pitcher, and poured it on the morning sacrifice as it lay upon the altar.

Q. What else did they during the continuance of this feast?

A. They carried in their hands branches of palm-trees, olives, citron, and myrtle, singing: "Hosannah!"—*i. e.*, "Save, I beseech thee." *Ps.* cxviii. 25.

Q. What else was done?

A. The city of Jerusalem was illuminated, and music, dancing, and feasting were the accompaniments of the festival.

Q. What does Josephus call this festival?

A. "A most holy and most eminent feast."

Q. What was done at this feast every seventh year?

A. The law of Moses was read in public in the presence of all the people.

Q. What incident in the life of the Saviour has reference to this feast?

A. On the day of his triumphal entry into Jerusalem, the believing Jews carried palms in their hands, singing, "Hosannah," to express their joy at finding in Him the fulfilment of all their hopes.

Q. What was the Feast of Trumpets?

A. It was the commencement of the civil year.

Q. From what did it derive its name?

A. From the blowing of trumpets in the Temple.

Q. When was it held?

A. On the first and second days of the month Tisri.

Q. What did the Jews on these days?

A. They abstained from labor, and offered particular sacrifices to God, which are described in Numbers, xxix. 6.

Lesson Forty-eighth.

THE DAY OF ATONEMENT.

Q. What was the Fast of Expiation, or Day of Atonement?

A. It was the most solemn and important of all the sacrifices ordained by the Mosaic law.

Q. When was it celebrated?

A. On the tenth day of the month Tisri, by the high-priest, for the sins of the nation.

Q. How was it observed by the people? *Lev.* xxiii. 27.

A. They abstained from all work, took no food, and afflicted their souls.

Q. What was the first duty of the high-priest on this day? *Lev.* xvi. 3, 4.

A. He first offered a sacrifice for himself, and the

priests and Levites, before he offered that for the people.

Q. What animals were offered on that day?

A. Two goats; one for a burnt-offering, and the other was presented alive unto the Lord. *Lev.* xvi. 21.

Q. What did the high-priest unto the live goat?

A. He put his hand on the goat's head, and confessed over him all the sins of Israel, and then sent him away into the Wilderness.

Q. What was this goat called?

A. The scape-goat.

Q. What did the high-priest with the blood of the goat which was sacrificed?

A. He took some of it into the inner sanctuary, and sprinkled it on the Mercy-seat.

Q. Who alone could make the atonement for sin?

A. The high-priest. *Lev.* xvi. 2, 17.

Q. Of what was this atonement a type?

A. It was a type of the great atonement which was afterwards made for the sins of the world by Jesus Christ, the "high-priest of our profession." *Heb.* iii. 1.

Q. What did the sending of the scape-goat into the Wilderness prefigure? *Isa.* liii. 4; *Matt* viii. 17.

A. It prefigured our Saviour, who was led by the

Holy Spirit into the wilderness, as the true scapegoat who bore away our infirmities.*

Q. What did the sacrifice of the other goat prefigure?

A. The death of Christ upon the cross, as the true sacrifice for sin.

Q. What other festivals did the Jews observe in later times? *Esther* ix. 26; *John*, x. 22.

A. The Feast of Purim and the Feast of Dedication.

Q. What was the Feast of Purim?

A. It commemorated the deliverance of the Jews from the plot of Haman, who had procured an edict from the king, Ahasuerus, to have them all massacred.

Q. When was the Feast of Purim celebrated?

A. On the fourteenth and fifteenth days of the month Adar, when the whole Book of Esther was read to the people. *Esth.* ix. 19.

Q. What else was done?

A. Alms were given to the poor; friends sent presents to each other; and they furnished their tables with every luxury that they could obtain.

---

* Horne's Introd., vol. ii., p. 127.

Lesson Forty-ninth.

FEAST OF DEDICATION AND SABBATICAL YEAR.

Q. What is the Feast of Dedication? 1 *Mac.* iv. 52, 59.

A. It was instituted by Judas Maccabeus, as a memorial of the cleansing of the second Temple, after it had been profaned by Antiochus.

Q. When was it celebrated?

A. It commenced on the twenty-fifth day of the month Cisleu, and lasted eight days.

Q. What was this festival also called?

A. The Feast of Lights, because the Jews illuminated their houses, in testimony of their joy and gladness.

Q. How was this feast celebrated?

A. In singing hymns, offering sacrifices, and in every kind of diversion.

Q. What was the Sabbatical year?

A. One year in seven, the people were forbidden to sow or reap the land, that the land might have rest.

Q. What was done with the spontaneous growth or produce of the seventh year?

A. It was devoted to charitable purposes, given to the wayfaring man and the stranger.

Q. How were the people supported during this year?

A. God promised that the land should bring forth a triple quantity the sixth year, so that there should be enough. *Lev.* xxv. 2, 22.

Q. What was the year of jubilee?

A. It was a more solemn sabbatical year, held every seventh sabbatical year.

Q. How often was that?

A. At the end of every forty-nine years, or the fiftieth current year.

Q. When did this festival begin? *Lev.* xxv. 9.

A. On the evening of the great day of atonement, which was the tenth day of the month Tisri.

Q. How was it proclaimed?

A. It was proclaimed by the sound of trumpets throughout the land.

Q. What was then proclaimed?

A. Liberty to slaves and captives, who were set free at once. *Lev.* xxv. 10.

Q. What was done in regard to debtors?

A. They were released from prison, and their debts cancelled.

Q. What law was made in regard to estates that had been sold?

A. They reverted to the original owners, so that no family should be reduced to perpetual poverty.

Q. What was the design of the law of the jubilee?

A. To prevent the too great oppression of the poor, as well as their liability to perpetual bondage.

Q. What typical design of the jubilee is pointed out by the prophet Isaiah?

A. Its reference to Christ, who "came to proclaim liberty to the captives, to bind up the broken-hearted, to open the eyes of the blind, and to proclaim the acceptable year of the Lord."

Lesson Fiftieth.

MINISTERS OF THE JEWISH CHURCH.

Q. Whom did God ordain to conduct the worship of the Jewish Church?

A. The tribe of Levi was especially devoted to this service.

Q. From what family of this tribe was the priesthood chosen?

A. From the family of Aaron, the rest of the tribe being employed in the inferior offices of the Temple.

Q. At what age did the Levites enter upon their duties in the Temple? *Num.* viii. 24, 25.

A. At the age of twenty-five years; and they continued to serve until fifty years of age.

Q. How many orders were there in the Jewish priesthood?

A. Three; the high-priest, the priests, and the Levites.

Q. What peculiar duty pertained to the office of the high-priest? *Num.* xxvii. 21.

A. The high-priest alone was the medium of communication between God and the people.

Q. What were the other duties of the high-priest?

A. The supreme administration of sacred things was confided to him; he was the judge of all controversies, and presided over the Sanhedrim.

Q. How was the high-priest inaugurated?

A. With great splendor; he was arrayed in the pontifical robes, and anointed with holy oil. *Exod.* xxix. 7, 8.

Q. How was the high-priest distinguished?

A. By a rich and glorious dress, adorned with gold and precious stones. *Exod.* xxviii. 4, 8.

Q. How was the high-priest supported?

A. By the offerings, and a portion of the sacrifice.

Q. What were the duties of the second order, the priests?

A. They offered the sacrifices, made the shewbread, and, morning and evening, burnt incense on the altar.

Q. What other duties did they perform? *Num.* vi. 23.

A. They blessed the people publicly, in the name of the Lord, and were the interpreters of the law.

Q. How were they supported?

A. By the offerings of the people; the first-fruits of their wine, corn, and oil, and of the flock.

Q. What were the duties of the third order, the Levites?

A. They assisted the priests in killing the sacrifice, sung and played on instruments in the Temple service, and distributed tithes.

Q. In what were the priests and Levites clothed during worship in the Temple? *Exod.* xxxix. 27.

A. "In white linen garments of woven work." *Ezek.* xliv. 17.

Q. What did God give the Levites to dwell in?

A. He gave them thirty-five cities, which, with thirteen for the priests, made in all forty-eight. *Josh.* xxi. 19, 41.

Lesson Fifty-first.

MEMBERS OF THE JEWISH CHURCH.

Q. Who were the first members of the Jewish Church?

A. Abraham and his family.

Q. What name did God give to Jacob?

A. He gave him the name of Israel. *Gen.* xxxii. 28.

Q. What were the descendants of Israel called?

A. Israelites, or the children of Israel, until the time of King Rehoboam, the son of Solomon.

Q. What happened then?

A. Ten of the tribes revolted, and were called the House of Israel, or Israelites.

Q. What two tribes remained faithful to the family of David?

A. Judah and Benjamin, which were called the House of Judah, or Jews.*

Q. Which of these two rebuilt the Temple?

A. Those who returned from the Babylonish captivity and rebuilt the Temple were Jews of the tribe of Judah, from which the Saviour was to come.

Q. How were persons admitted into the Jewish Church?

A. By circumcision, and by baptism.

Q. What was circumcision?

A. It was the seal of the covenant by which infants and proselytes were received into the Church of God.

Q. What was the Jewish baptism?

A. The washing or sprinkling of a person with water, in the presence of at least three Jews of distinction, accompanied by a solemn profession on the part of the person baptized.

---

* Horne's Introd., vol. ii., p. 108.

Q. What did the person promise?

A. To lead a holy life, to worship the true God, and to keep his commandments.

Q. Were the children of Gentile converts also baptized?

A. Yes; generally at the same time as their parents.

Q. What other ceremony was performed at the same time?

A. That of offering sacrifices.

Q. Did the Jews receive idolaters and heathen into the Church, on their renunciation of their idolatry?

A. Yes; they admitted them to their services, but would not allow them to participate in their sacred rites.

Q. On what conditions did they receive a proselyte?

A. A person must come *voluntarily*, no influence being permitted; and he must separate himself from all his former friends.

Q. What other conditions were made?

A. He must agree to bear patiently the yoke of the Jewish Church, and the sufferings which his new profession might bring upon him, and engage to continue faithful to the Jewish Church unto death.

Q. Did proselytes eat the Passover? *Num.* ix. 14.

A. Yes; and the man who refused to eat the Passover was punished with death.

Q. At what age were children permitted to partake of the Passover? *Luke*, ii. 42.

A. At the age of twelve years.

Lesson Fifty-second.

SACRIFICES.

Q. What was one of the principal services of the Jewish Church?

A. The offering of sacrifices and oblations.

Q. What was a sacrifice?

A. It was a free-will offering made to God by the hand of a lawful minister.

Q. What was an oblation?

A. It was a simple gift.

Q. What was the difference between a sacrifice and an oblation?

A. In the sacrifice there was a change or destruction of the thing offered, whereas an oblation was merely a gift.

Q. How many kinds of sacrifices were there?

A. Four; burnt-offerings, peace-offerings, sin-offerings, and trespass-offerings.

Q. What was a burnt-offering?

A. An animal without blemish was brought to the altar, slain there, and the blood caught in a vessel and sprinkled upon the altar.

Q. What was next done?

A. The animal was cut into quarters, and a portion of it burned upon the altar, where a fire was always kept burning. *Lev.* vi. 13.

Q. What animals were used in burnt sacrifices?

A. Animals of the ox kind, goats and sheep, turtle doves and pigeons.

Q. What was signified by the sprinkling of the blood upon the altar?

A. That an atonement had been made for sin.

Q. What did these sacrifices prefigure?

A. The atonement made by the sacrifice of Christ, who died for the sins of the world.

Q. What was Christ called?

A. "The Lamb of God which taketh away the sin of the world."

Q. What were peace-offerings? *Lev.* iii. 1.

A. They were free-will offerings in token of peace and reconciliation between God and man.

Q. Of what did these offerings consist?

A. Of animals, or of bread or dough.*

Q. How were they offered?

---

* Horne's Introd., vol. ii., p. 118.

A. A part was burnt on the altar, and the rest was eaten by the priest and the party offering it.

Q. What was a sin-offering? *Lev.* iv.

A. It was a sacrifice offered for sins committed through ignorance.

Q. How did the sin-offering differ from others?

A. The priest sprinkled the blood on the horns of the altar, and the fat only was burnt upon the altar, and the rest of the animal was burnt without the camp. *Lev.* iv. 18, 19, 21.

Lesson Fifty-third.

SACRIFICES—CONTINUED.

Q. What was a trespass-offering? *Lev.* v. 17, 18.

A. It was made when the person offering had violated the law of God, though unconscious of it at the time.

Q. How did the trespass-offering differ from a sin-offering? *Lev.* vi. 30; vii. 6.

A. The sin-offering was to be burnt with fire, and not allowed to be eaten; the trespass-offering was to be eaten by the priests after the fat had been burnt.

Q. What were meat-offerings? *Lev.* ii. 1, 14.

A. They were taken wholly from the vegetable kingdom, and were of fine flour, oil, frankincense, and ears of corn.

Q. When could these be presented as offerings for sin?

A. Only when the person was too poor to bring two doves or pigeons.

Q. Why were two doves to be offered?

A. One was for a sin-offering, the other for a burnt-offering. *Lev.* v. 9, 10.

Q. How often were sacrifices offered in the Temple?

A. The daily sacrifice was offered morning and evening, the weekly sacrifice on every Sabbath-day in addition, and the monthly sacrifice on every new moon

Q. What others besides these?

A. The yearly sacrifices; which were offered on the great festivals.

Q. What was the drink-offering?

A. It was wine; part of which was poured on the brow of the victim, and part was given to the priests, who drank it with their portion of the sacrifice.

Q. How many kinds of oblations were there?

A. Three; ordinary, prescribed, and voluntary.

Q. What were the ordinary oblations?

A. The shew-bread and incense.

Q. What was the shew-bread?

A. Twelve loaves; which were placed hot every Sabbath day upon the golden table in the Sanctuary.

Q. What was incense? *Exod.* xxx. 34.

A. It consisted of fragrant spices, stacte, onycha, galbanum, and frankincense, an equal quantity of each, which was burnt morning and evening on a golden altar.

Q. What were voluntary oblations?

A. They were the fruits of promises or vows.

Q. What were prescribed oblations?

A. They were offerings which all persons were obliged to bring of the first-fruits of their corn, wine, oil, and fruits, which were consecrated to God.

Q What else were Jews obliged to give for the worship of God?

A. Besides the first-fruits, they gave a tenth of their income for the year.

Lesson Fifty-fourth.

VOWS AND PRAYERS.

Q. What was the nature of the vows which the Jews made?

A. They were promises made to God voluntarily, but which could be enforced by the priest. *Deut.* xxiii. 23, 24.

Q. What is the earliest vow spoken of in the Bible?

A. It is that of Jacob, when he vowed to give a tenth of all he possessed to the Lord. *Gen.* xxviii. 22.

Q. What was required of things devoted to God?

A. That they should be the best of the kind which the person offering possessed. *Mal.* i. 8.

Q. Could a vow be redeemed?

A. In certain cases, Moses permitted the annulling of a vow. *Lev.* xxvii. 1, 25.

Q. How were vows uttered? *Num.* xxx. 11.

A. They were uttered audibly, and confirmed by an oath.

Q. How many sorts of vows were there?

A. Two; the Cherem and the Nederim.*

Q. What was the first—the Cherem?

A. It was the most solemn, and could not be redeemed.

Q. What was this vow sometimes called?

A. "The irrevocable curse;" and it was generally uttered in respect to enemies, and was designed to bear only upon the wicked.

Q. What furnishes an example of this vow?

A. The history of the taking of the city of Jericho by the Israelites, under Joshua.

---

* Horne's Introd., vol. ii., p. 130.

Q. Describe it. *Josh.* vi. 17, 19, 21, 24.

A. The city was accursed by Joshua, because he intended to destroy it utterly. No booty was allowed; the silver and gold were devoted to the Sanctuary, and every thing else was burnt to the ground.

Q. What were the Nederim, or common vows?

A. They were vows of dedication, and vows of abstinence.

Q. Give an example of the first vow. *Num.* xxi. 3.

A. A person would promise to bring an offering to God.

Q. What was the vow of abstinence?

A. The person vowed to abstain from some article of food, or some other thing.

Q. What was the custom of the devout Jews in regard to prayer?

A. They usually prayed three times a day. *Dan.* vi. 10.

Q. What were their times of prayer called?

A. Public, private, and stated hours of prayer.

Q. What were the public prayers?

A. Those offered in the Temple and synagogues by the priest.

Q. What were private prayers? *Luke*, xviii. 13.

A. Those offered by individuals, in a low voice, by themselves, in the Temple or elsewhere.

Q. What were the stated hours of prayer?

A. The times of offering the morning and evening sacrifice.

Q. What fast was instituted by Moses?

A. He instituted but one public fast, that of the Day of Atonement.

Q. Were any other fasts observed? 1 *Sam.* vii. 5, 6; 2 *Chron.* xx. 3.

A. Occasional fasts were appointed by the civil magistrates.

Q. How did the Jews keep their fasts?

A. They clothed themselves with sackcloth, put ashes on their heads, and rent their garments.

Lesson Fifty-fifth.

PURIFICATIONS OF THE JEWS.

Q. What were the Jews obliged to do before they could offer an acceptable sacrifice to God?

A. They were obliged to purify themselves.

Q. What was the design of these purifications?

A. To inculcate the necessity of inward purity, and also to preserve the health and morals of the Jews.

Q. How were these purifications performed?

A. Sometimes by dipping the hands and feet in

water; sometimes by sprinkling with blood, or anointing with oil. *Lev.* viii. 10; *Heb.* ix. 21.

Q. What was sometimes mixed with the water?

A. The ashes of a red heifer. *Num.* xix. 3, 9.

Q. How was the sprinkling performed? *Lev.* xiv. 4, 6.

A. Either with the finger, or with a branch of hyssop and cedar, tied together with scarlet wool.

Q. How were priests purified before their consecration? *Ex.* xxix. 4.

A. They were washed with water.

Q. How often were they obliged to purify themselves?

A. Every time they went into the Tabernacle or Temple to offer sacrifices or prayers. *Exod.* xxx. 20.

Q. How were the Tabernacle and sacred vessels purified?

A. They were anointed with oil, or sprinkled with blood.

Q. What constituted uncleanness, and required purification also?

A. Touching a dead body, touching a leper or the dead body of an animal that had died of disease, and other things mentioned in Lev. xii. to xvi.

Q. What was the result of this law in regard to dead animals?

A. The bodies of beasts were buried immediately, that passers-by might not be injured.

Q. What good effect had these wise enactments?

A. The spreading of contagious diseases was prevented, which, in hot climates, are peculiarly rapid and fatal.

Q. What rule was made in regard to earthen vessels which had been left in a tent where a person had died?

A. They were to be broken, in order to avoid contagion.

Q. Were the priests also bound to obey all these laws?

A. Yes; the high-priests, priests, and Levites were commanded to purify, not only themselves, but their clothes, before executing their respective offices.

Q. What were tithes?

A. A tenth part of all one's produce or gains was devoted to the Lord.

Q. Where is the first mention made of tithes? *Gen.* xiv. 20.

A. Abraham gave to Melchisedek, the priest of the most high God, tithes of all he had taken from the enemy.

Q. By whom were the tithes collected and disbursed?

A. By the Levites.

Q. What were also consecrated to God?

A. The first fruits of corn, wine, oil, and of the flock were considered sacred unto the Lord.

Lesson Fifty-sixth.

IDOLATRIES OF THE JEWS.

Q. What is idolatry?

A. It is the superstitious worship of idols or false gods.

Q. Where is idolatry first spoken of in Scripture?

A. Laban, the father-in-law of Jacob, was an idolater. *Gen.* xxxi. 30.

Q. What did the Israelites while they were in Egypt?

A. They worshipped the deities of Egypt. *Josh.* xxiv. 14.

Q. What did they after their departure from Egypt?

A. While Moses was in the mount, the people caused Aaron to make them a golden calf, which they worshipped.

Q. What did the Jews again after the death of Joshua?

A. They worshipped the gods of the Canaanites, Baal and Ashtaroth. *Judges* ii. 12 13.

Q. What else did the Jews worship?

A. The brazen serpent, which was preserved as a monument of the Divine mercy, was afterwards worshipped as a god.

Q. What idols were made by Jeroboam, the first king of Israel, after the secession of the ten tribes?

A. Two golden calves, which he set up at Dan and Bethel.

Q. What were Teraphim? 1 *Sam.* xix. 13.

A. They were carved images, in human form, and household deities.

Q. Who was Moloch? 1 *Kings,* xi. 7.

A. He was the principal idol of the Ammonites, to whom Solomon wickedly built a temple on the Mount of Olives, in his old age.

Q. Who was Baal P'eor, spoken of in Numbers, xxv. 1, 5.

A. He was a deity worshipped by the Moabites and is supposed to be the same as Chemosh, to whom Solomon also erected an altar on the Mount of Olives.

Q. Who was Rimmon? 2 *Kings,* v. 18.

A. Rimmon was an idol of the Syrians, but not worshipped by the Israelites.

Q. What was Ashtaroth? *Judges,* ii. 13.

A. It was the moon, worshipped by the Jews at one time.

Q. Who was Baal, mentioned in connection with Ashtaroth?

A. He was one of the chief of the heathen deities, also worshipped by the Jews.

Q. Who was Dagon? *Judges*, xvi. 23.

A. He was the god of the Philistines, the people of Ashdod.

Q. Who was Baal-berith? *Judges*, viii. 33.

A. He was the idol of the Shechemites.

Q. Who were Bel and Nebo, spoken of by Isaiah, xlvi. 1?

A. They were Babylonian deities.

Q. What were idols made of?

A. At first, they were made of wood and stone; afterwards, of ivory and metal.

Q. What were those made of wood covered with?

A. "They were covered with laminæ of gold and silver, or were clothed with precious vests."*

Q. What were the principal parts of the idol worship?

A. Sacrifices, prayers, and festivals, and purifications.

Q. Of what did the sacrifices consist?†

A. Of salt, honey, incense, cakes, beasts, and men. By the Canaanites, the most promising of their children were sacrificed. *Deut.* xviii. 10.

---

* Jahn's Arch., p. 509. † Ibid., p. 511.

Lesson Fifty-seventh.

JEWISH SECTS.

Q. Were there any sects among the Jews before the captivity?

A. No; not until the time of the Maccabees.

Q. What were the principal sects among the Jews?

A. The Pharisees, the Sadducees, and the Essenes.

Q. When were they first known?

A. Josephus says "they were distinct sects in the reign of Jonathan," B. C. 144.

Q. What is known of the Pharisees?

A. They were the most numerous and powerful of the Jewish sects, and made great pretensions to peculiar holiness. *Luke*, xviii. 11.

Q. Did they belong to any particular tribe?

A. No; there were Pharisees of every tribe and every family.

Q. What were some of their peculiar tenets or doctrines?

A. They ascribed all things to fate, believed in the existence of angels and spirits, in the resurrection of the dead, and the transmigration of souls.*

---

* Horne's Introd., vol. ii., p. 144.

Q. What effect had the latter doctrine on the minds of the Jews in regard to Christ?

A. They thought the soul of Elias or Jeremiah might have been in the body of Jesus Christ.

Q. What is said of the Sadducees?

A. They are supposed to be the most ancient of the Jewish sects.

Q. What were the principal tenets of the Sadducees?

A. They denied the resurrection of the body and the existence of angels or spirits, and maintained that the soul of man died with the body.

Q. Mention other things that they denied, which were believed by the Pharisees.

A. They did not believe in an overruling Providence, or in the traditions of the Pharisees, but kept strictly to the letter of the Scriptures.

Q. Was the sect numerous?

A. No; in point of numbers, it was small.

Q. What was the third principal sect?

A. The Essenes.

Q. What was their character?

A. They were moral, abstemious, exemplary in every way, and very rigid in their observance of the Sabbath.

Q. What were their tenets?

A. They believed in the immortality of the soul, and in future rewards and punishments, but denied the resurrection of the body.

Q. How did the Essenes live?

A. They held their property in common, and things which were needed were distributed from the common stock.*

Q. What were the Zealots? *Num.* xxv. 6-13; 1 *Mac.* ii. 24, 25.

A. An association of persons, who undertook to maintain the purity of Divine worship by inflicting punishments, without form of trial, upon all who violated any institution which they held sacred.

Lesson Fifty-eighth.

JEWISH SECTS—CONCLUDED.

Q. Who were the Scribes, spoken of in the time of Christ?

A. They were the persons who transcribed the law, and took their name from that employment.

Q. Were they a sect by themselves?

A. No; they were of different sects; some were Pharisees, and some were Sadducees.

Q. Who were the Hellenists?*

---

* Jahn's Arch., pp. 410, 411.

A. They were the Jews who, not only in Asia Minor, and Greece, and Egypt, but in all places, spoke the Greek language.

Q. Who were the lawyers?

A. Some persons suppose them to have been the Scribes; others think they were a distinct class of men, who expounded the text of the law, and disregarded all traditions.

Q. What were Proselytes?

A. They were persons, once idolaters, who had been converted to the Jewish Church; and both men and women were baptized in the presence of three witnesses.

Q. Who were the Samaritans?

A. They were a race of people composed of the descendants of the ten tribes, and some of the Gentile nations, with whom they had intermarried.

Q. What did they desire, on the return of the tribe of Judah from the captivity?

A. They wanted to be acknowledged as Jewish citizens, and to be permitted to assist in rebuilding the Temple.

Q. What was the result of the application?

A. It was rejected by the Jews of the tribe of Judah, and a bitter enmity sprang up in consequence.

Q. What did the Samaritans then?

A. They built a temple on Mount Gerizim; and

the national hatred grew to such a height, that all intercourse ceased between them.

Q. Was their worship like that of the Jews?

A. Yes; they kept the Sabbath and the Passover; but they worshipped idols also.*

Q. Who were the Herodians?

A. They were a political faction, rather than a religious sect, and derived their name from Herod the Great.

Q. What were their doctrinal tenets?

A. They were chiefly those of the Sadducees, who were the most indifferent to religion of all the Jews.

Q. How were the Herodians distinguished from other Jewish sects?

A. They copied the Romans in many of their heathen practices, such as erecting temples for idolatrous worship.

Q. Who were the Galileans?

A. They were a political sect, that originated from the Pharisees, and they endeavored to shake off the Roman yoke by refusing to pay tribute to Rome.

---

* Jahn's Arch.

www.ingramcontent.com/pod-product-compliance
Lightning Source LLC
Chambersburg PA
CBHW030436190426
43202CB00036B/1316